Solution Training

Solution Training

Overcoming Blocks in Problem Solving

James R. Baugh

PELICAN PUBLISHING COMPANY

GRETNA 1980

Library of Congress Cataloging in Publication Data

Baugh, James R.
  Solution training.

  Bibliography: p.
  1. Problem solving. 2. Success. I. Title.
BF441.B34   158'.1   79–20717
ISBN 0-88289-246-0

Manufactured in the United States of America

Published by Pelican Publishing Company, Inc.
630 Burmaster Street, Gretna, Louisiana 70053

Designed by Mike Burton

Contents

Figures

To my children:
Jay, David, Bobby, and Becky

Acknowledgements

I wish to acknowledge the contributions of my teachers, both instructors and clients. Special gratitude goes to Elaine Henry for her personal support, encouragement, and editorial contribution.

Introduction

Before You Begin

For years after I began my education in psychology, I asked my professors and other "experts," "What is psychotherapy?" The answers I received turned out to be "pieces of the total elephant" and therefore only partially satisfying.

"Psychotherapy is total acceptance of the other person, allowing him to grow," I was told. "Psychotherapy is behavior change through contingently reinforcing those behaviors that are useful and extinguishing those that are not useful," a second opinion. "Psychotherapy is correcting irrational thinking." "Psychotherapy is analyzing the transference phenomenon." And so forth.

One consistent factor unites all of the theories—psychotherapy involves change. Change is necessary because what those of us seeking therapy are doing in our lives is not meeting our needs. The change that takes place, when therapeutic, is related to the problem of our unfulfilled needs or wants. We change what we think, feel, or do to meet our goals or to get what we want out of life. The world around us is in a constant state of change. The greatest power we have is *the power to change* ourselves to meet the new conditions around us. When a problem exists, we must change ourselves to solve the problem or we may remain passive and hope it goes away.

My own definition of psychotherapy is *training others to improve their problem-solving skills*. Sometimes teaching "pieces of the elephant" relates to solving the problem at hand, sometimes not. At other times, accepting feelings or changing behavior or revising thinking misses the key to a solution when experienced as isolated occurrences.

Psychotherapy then is a training procedure in which we learn to improve our own problem-solving skills, to act as our own change agents, and eventually to be our own psychotherapists. The essence of good problem solving is to avoid a passive position—which leads us to believe we are blocked, causing us to give up seeking a solution. *All problems have a solution*, although the particular way we have defined our problems or the actions we have considered may not necessarily lead to solutions. New definitions and new actions will eventually relieve our discomfort.

Solution Training

Chapter 1

 Why Are Problems Such
Problems? Your Basic
Wants and Needs

He was depressed, although he was a reflective and intelligent individual. Leaning back in his chair, he began
to tell me about a portion of his life philosophy: "If I
say I want to do well—to win—and then I lose, I'm sad.
If I say I want to do poorly, or lose, and I lose, then I
got what I said I wanted; but that's nothing. So I figure
the best way to avoid disappointment is to want nothing—zero—not to win, excel, achieve, be loved, or live."

"Then you'll never get what you really want," I suggested to him.

Hesitantly he began, "Then how . . . "

And there began solution training, a structured approach to psychotherapy that identifies blocks to problem solving and systematically guides the trainee to
workable solutions. In the above example, and with
many of my clients, this troubled individual is in a corner. He is damned if he works toward goals without
perfect achievement; he is damned if he gives up because he never gets his needs met. He may think he is
in a corner because "try, try again" doesn't work for

1

him, but in reality the corner is of his own construction—in fact, no corner at all. My client has defined his problem so that no solution is possible. He will learn to redefine with a definition that points to a positive action.

Wants and Needs

How do you or I know that we have a problem? We generally become aware that a problem exists when we discover that what we are doing is not working well. The "not working" means that our actions fail to result in need satisfaction. Generally, behavior is initiated to fulfill a need or want. When our needs persist and our present actions do not yield satisfaction, we experience discomfort and realize that a *problem* exists.

Upon awareness of the discomfort, it is important that we be able to identify what need or want is being denied. In clinical practice, and somewhat less frequently in management consultation, I have found that many of us experience discomfort and realize a problem exists, yet we are unaware of what we need or want. The first two steps in problem identification call for us to define: (1) the current circumstances that are dissatisfying to us and (2) the circumstances that we believe will be satisfying in the future when problem solving is completed.

The first question, related to "what's happening now" that we don't like, is generally one that most of us easily identify. However, the second question, related to what we want in the future, is usually vague and not clearly defined. That is, we may be willing to launch into a problem-solving effort without knowing where we are going or what we expect when the solution is found. Consider Lewis Carroll's *Alice in Wonderland*:

"Cheshire Puss . . . Would you tell me please, which way I ought to walk from here?"

"That depends a good deal on where you want to get," said the Cat.

"I don't much care where," said Alice.

"Then it doesn't matter which way you walk," said the Cat.

Of my clients, those who are least likely to know what they need or want are the ones who have spent a lifetime working toward other people's goals—not toward their own. These individuals put heavy emphasis on pleasing others and have not thought much about their own wants, desires, or needs. It is both logical and necessary that individuals know what they want or where they want to be at the end of their problem-solving sequence before they begin a problem-solving plan.

What a person *needs* (basic to survival or a full life experience) or *wants* (learned desires) is a source of human motivation. According to Clark L. Hull's learning theory, basic needs are experienced as a drive state (uncomfortable feeling) in the individual. This uncomfortable state is reduced upon need satisfaction, and the behaviors involved in drive reduction are reinforced, thereby becoming learned habits.

Two writers have organized the concept of human needs, or drives, into understandable structures that can easily be related to human experience. Both writers, Eric Berne and Abraham Maslow, describe needs but develop their ideas from slightly different perspectives. Maslow's construction of "basic needs" is the more comprehensive and includes the socially oriented approach of Berne's "hungers."

Eric Berne's basic "hungers" include the need for sensory stimulation (sight, taste, sound, touch, smell) or *stimulus-hunger*. This basic need is well documented in experimental psychology. Animals, when stimulus deprived, develop physical and behavioral-social deficits.

Stimulus-hunger, in time, is replaced (partially) by *recognition-hunger* as the infant grows into a child. We never lose the need for recognition for ourselves or our actions. The recognition may be either positive or negative. That is, although we may prefer a compliment, we would rather be criticized than ignored. Recognition includes any form of communication signaling that "somebody else is there" who recognizes our existence either for what we are or for what we are doing.

Berne calls each unit of recognition a *stroke*. Because the concept of stroking is an important therapeutic and interpersonal tool, I will explore the idea further at this point. We may receive positive regard for being ourselves or for specific behaviors, or we may receive negative regard for either. Such regard may lead to a positive unconditional statement, "I love you," or a positive conditional statement, "I like it when you do that." On the other hand, negative regard may be expressed as a negative unconditional statement, "I hate you and everything you stand for," or a negative conditional statement, "I don't like it when you do that." The unconditional strokes are for *being*. The conditional strokes are for *doing*.

Deprivation of stroking needs results in both physical and psychological deficits; the degree of these deficits corresponds to the degree of deprivation. While in a navy training school, I had the opportunity to witness the effect of the "silent treatment" given to one of the sailors who had been excessively harassing others in the program. The other 150 men decided to stop recognizing his existence. We would "look through him" and not respond to any approach he made. In two days, this once-forceful man was reduced to tears.

Berne's next hunger is the need to structure our waking hours to avoid boredom, or *structure-hunger*. Berne divides the possible ways of structuring time into the following six categories: withdrawal, rituals, activities, pastimes, games, and intimacy. These ways of spending time will be discussed in Chapter 8.

Maslow views our basic needs in hierarchical levels. Each level must be satisfied before the next is confronted. Maslow's first level comprises *biological needs* (food, water, air). Next is the *need to feel safe*, to be free of fears. A sense of safety is followed by a *social need* to interact with others. Successful social need satisfaction resolves into a need for *self-esteem*, a self-respectful pride for our accomplishments. The top of the hierarchy is *self-actualization*, which is a somewhat vague, existential state of being in which full potential is achieved.

A combined hierarchy derived from both Maslow's and Berne's structures is as follows:

1. *Biological needs.* The need for food, water, air, sex, moderate temperature, sensory stimulation
2. *Safety.* The need to be free of fear
3. *Social.* The need to structure time to interact with other human beings by giving and receiving social recognition and to avoid boredom
4. *Self-esteem.* The need for self-respect and pride in our accomplishments
5. *Self-actualization.* The need to achieve our potential

The hierarchical effect is exemplified by those of us

who say that we want self-respect but then hinder ourselves from satisfying this higher need—chiefly because we have not created a basic sense of safety in our environment. For example, we may feel safe only when we are pleasing other people. By focusing on pleasing others and achieving others' wants, we prevent ourselves from focusing on our own personal growth and self-respect. By wanting to please others, we don't have a clear idea of what we personally need or want. We have not felt the safety to explore, take risks, and become aware of our own desires. Pleasing others, when it is possible, is only partially satisfying.

In order to be efficient problem solvers, we must identify our needs and wants to aid in goal setting. If we do not know what we want, we have no direction. We do not know where to scratch if we have not located the itch.

Some of us, in looking for what we need, confuse means and ends. It is important to distinguish means from ends because there are many different means— of varying degrees of accessibility—to a particular end. Some things we think we need are actually a means to an end (a basic need). "I need a new house," you may state. A new house may in fact be a means of satisfying a need for self-esteem. However, distinguishing means from ends allows you to choose another action to satisfy your need for self-esteem. This is especially important if a new house is not attainable.

Those of us who persist in failing to find out what our needs are may have decided early that we can never know what we need or want. I once oserved a little girl being told by her mother that she wasn't hungry when she expressed a desire to eat, and then a short time later being told by her father that she wasn't feeling too cold when she complained about the temperature.

Such training may continue into later life, leading to a situation exemplified by the following incident that I observed at a party. A couple, married for about twenty years, were sitting on a couch. The hostess approached and asked the man if he would like a coke. He replied, "I don't know," and turned to his wife. "Honey, do I want a coke?"

His wife thought for a few seconds and answered, "No, I don't think so tonight."

He turned to the hostess and replied, "No thank you."

Incredible as this may sound, relationships can develop into this kind of symbiosis when one partner is excessively deficient in defining his or her own needs and wants.

How We Usually Meet Our Needs

Most of our day-to-day needs are satisfied by habits; without conscious decision, we follow a well-established pattern of behavior. We learn these habits by trial and error and by modeling after others. The resulting behavior pattern was thus learned originally to bring about need satisfaction.

The future brings new conditions in which these old habits are ineffectual in achieving need satisfaction. The result is discomfort. As good problem solvers we use the discomfort to motivate ourselves to identify our problems and make new decisions about our behavior under the changed conditions.

Problem solving, or finding something that works to

get our needs met in areas where we have not developed habits, generally follows a more or less systematic, trial-and-error method as follows:

1. Decide what the problem is.
2. Think about the problem and actions to take to solve the problem.
3. Take action.
4. Evaluate the results of the action taken.
5. Repeat steps 2 and 3, modifying and refining your actions until the problem is solved to your satisfaction.

The above steps are those taken by most of us, in some form, to solve our problems.

A more formal outline of good problem-solving procedure is as follows:

1. *Feel discomfort.* Every problem is initiated by some discomfort on our part.
2. *Recognize the problem.* We must recognize that the discomfort is signaling a problem to be solved.
3. *Define a solvable problem.* In order to deal with the awareness of a problem in an effective manner, a definition must organize and structure the conceived problem in such a manner that an action can be taken to relieve the discomfort.
4. *Accept responsibility.* We must accept that it is our responsibility to solve the problem and be responsible for our behavior, thoughts, and feelings in achieving a solution.
5. *Think of an action.* We must think of an action that has a probability of solving the problem without causing more discomfort than the solution relieves.
6. *Take action.* All problem solving must involve action to get needs met.

7. *Evaluate.* To be successful problem solvers, we evaluate the effectiveness of our actions. If we judge them a success, then the sequence ends with a solution. If we judge them a failure, a recycling begins with either a new definition or a new action or both until the problem is solved.

But what happens when we get stuck somewhere in the process?

Problem-Solving Blocks

Problem solving is a learned skill. Faulty experience leads to poor problem-solving behaviors and sets up blocks that prevent or obscure actions which would result in a solution. Any of the following blocks in the flow of normal problem solving places you, the solver, in a passive position, choosing passive behaviors not helpful in getting your need met. When in a passive position, your problems accumulate and your discomfort increases. The increased bad feeling leads you (since you are blocked in solving your problem) to manipulate other people to solve your problem for you. In the final stages you may become completely incapacitated, thereby forcing someone else to take care of you.

Recognition blocks occur when you do not know what you want or need or what's bugging you. You may keep these data from yourself by distorting reality. (The methods of distortion are discussed in Chapter 4.) We all distort reality from time to time, to maintain our belief system. Our belief system is the *major block in solving problems*. If recognizing the existence of a problem transgresses a belief, we will distort reality and keep the problem from awareness. Our belief system and the distortion that protects the beliefs are so important as blocking agents that they enter into every other problem-solving block. Your belief system contains decisions that become rules by which you live. These rules will be defended even when they cause need deprivation, if breaking the rule causes an even greater discomfort than the unsatisfied need. A good deal of time and energy is invested in your belief system, and you will distort reality in the service of maintaining a consistency in what you believe.

Defining blocks result from lack of knowledge and skill training in defining problems. Our education system contributes only vaguely to good problem definitions. Again your belief system will cause distortions in defining if a basic rule must be broken to define the problem in a solvable manner. The particular definition given may point to no solution, an easy solution, or a difficult one.

Responsibility blocks occur when you choose not to "own the problem." You give away this responsibility to resolve your discomfort. Even if you accept that the problem is yours to solve, you may not accept responsibility for your behavior, feelings, and thoughts, which may block a solution. For example, a problem solver states, "I would solve my marital problems, but my wife keeps on *making me mad* and I can't get to the problem." The solver gives away responsibility and control of his feeling and therefore remains blocked.

Thinking blocks are only slightly related to intelligence. Intelligence sets a limit on the ability to develop ideas of what action to take; however, most of my clients are blocked by their own rules about thinking, or they may be trapped in their own logical system. For example, some bright individuals have made the decision to get other people to do their thinking for them. Their rule is: "Don't think. Get someone else to do it for you, or at least check out and validate any thinking you do for yourself." The second block involves people who are logical and clear thinkers. However, all their good logic has not generated a workable action. They will continue to be blocked if they do not break out of their own logic and get a new perspective on the problem.

Action blocks include two major areas. You may lack basic information or skill necessary in taking action. For example, you may recognize that you must control your emotions to reach a solution, but you may not know how to do the controlling. Other skill deficits blocking action might include: time management, emotional awareness (as in the above example), self-management, and assertive communication skills.

A second action block involves the unwillingness to choose an action to take. You may be a good thinker and able to generate many workable alternatives yet take no action. You may avoid making a decision because you burden yourself with the belief that you have to make the "right choice." Your problem is that the measure of "rightness" rests on observable results of the action taken. If you delay action until you are certain of the absolute correctness of your decision, you may never do anything about your problem except worry.

Evaluation blocks are heavily tied in with your belief system and your distortions to protect what you believe. As a blocked solver, you may repeat the same action over and over, ignoring the failure to relieve your distress because you believe your action is the "right thing to do." An example is a parent who continues a particular kind of discipline in spite of the lack of effect on his child because "that's the way his daddy did it and it's the right thing to do."

Blockbusting

Breaking through the above blocks involves ten steps in the teaching and training of problem-solving technique—solution training. In essence, solution training is designed to complement your current level of problem-solving skills. Therefore, one person may need solution training from Step I, while another will start at Step III.

In Figure 1 the outline reveals how and where solution training fits into the problem-solving process. Each block has a corresponding training procedure. The intervention techniques are described in the last chapter of this book.

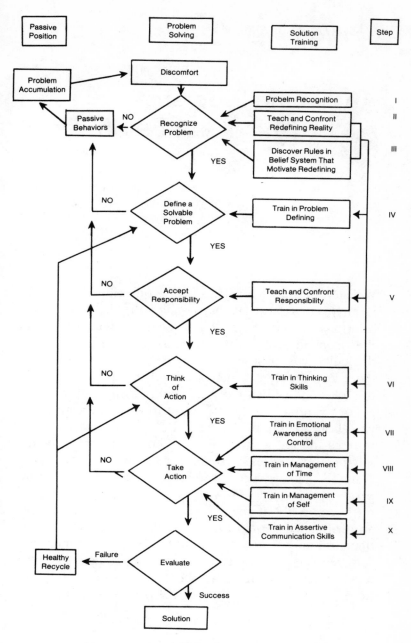

Figure 1
PROBLEM SOLVING AND SOLUTION TRAINING

Chapter 2

Define Problems
So They Can Be Solved

Webster defines a problem as "a question raised for inquiry, consideration, or *solution*." Problems do have solutions if you as a problem solver correctly identify the problem and define the situation you are having difficulty with in a *solvable manner*. The reverse is also true: any problem can be defined in such a way that the solution is much more difficult, or impossible.

For example, I presently want to communicate with you about solving problems. If I define my task as communicating by writing what I know about problem solving and organizing that information according to a generally agreed upon set of grammatical rules, my problem is solvable. However, if I set my goal as communicating about my subject in such eloquent prose and with such depth of meaning that everyone will understand and accept my ideas, then I have significantly reduced the probability of successful problem solving.

As another example, a colleague of mine stated (as he saw me writing a chapter on problem solving), "I

14

have a problem with getting my paper work done."

"Will you define the problem you are working on?"
I asked him.

"My problem is that I need to find out how to make myself do the damned paper work, and I hate it every time I start."

From the way my friend has defined his problem, what is your own hunch about the probability of his being successful in finding a solution?

Most likely his definition will result in his doing paper work only under strong outside demands. He will make himself do it with a great deal of effort involved in overcoming his desire to avoid doing what he hates. In other words, he will procrastinate until the last possible minute. My hope for him is that, after he reads this chapter, he will define his problem in a more solvable manner.

In my seminars on problem solving, participants usually take issue with the generalization that all problems have solutions. A middle-aged woman stated, "My problem is that I want a twenty-two-inch waist." A man queried, "What about a person in a wheelchair? He can't solve his problem of not being able to walk."

Facts of life are not problems to be solved. There are thousands of potential problems facing us daily, and we choose what to focus on. Both the middle-aged woman and the handicapped person have problems of how to get recognition from those close to them and how to get their daily needs met. Should the above people choose to focus on "walking" or "reducing middle-aged spread to high school size," they are not problem solving. Rather, they are needlessly setting themselves up to fail.

Both the man and the woman above have the option of redefining their problems. For example, the woman may restate her problem as learning to set realistic goals or learning to avoid unnecessary suffering. All problems have a solution; the distress causing them can be reduced if we are willing to redefine them in a solvable manner. *All problems do have solutions. However, a particular problem definition may block a workable solution.*

"What about creativity and scientific discovery?" someone asks. The recognition of facts of life is not intended to discourage progress or to limit personal growth. If a researcher wants to solve a problem with no known solution, he may define his problem as the development of a research technique to test his assumptions regarding the area of inquiry. He now has defined a problem with a probable solution.

Creative problem definitions give the problem solver a direction and some action to take. Unproductive definitions leave the individual helpless to respond.

For the purposes of this book, a problem is defined as an event or situation producing discomfort for which we have not developed an automatic response habit to get our needs met. We must therefore consciously develop a strategy from experience to meet these needs, thereby reducing our discomfort.

Human beings are excellent problem-solving machines. We have sensory apparatus that puts us in contact with most of the relevant stimuli in our environment. We have an enormous capacity to learn from our experience. Our language helps us abstract and organize what we have learned into meaningful problem-solving tools. Our body is capable of both gross and fine motor skills in acting upon the environment.

You are already solving hundreds of problems daily in a satisfactory manner. This book can assist in finding solutions to those relatively few persistent problems that do not yield to your current problem-solving skills.

Recognizing Problems

The first step in changing a problematic situation is recognizing the problem. A problem will not likely be solved if the parameters are poorly defined or misstated. J. L. Schiff, discussing discounts that interfere with problem solving, points out that problem identification begins with awareness of a stimulus. If, for example, a manager is unaware of an angry look on the face of his secretary, he will inquire no further into a matter that may or may not be a problem to him. And if he denies that his own jaws are tightened and that his heart rate is accelerating, he may never deal with the problem that is inviting his own anger.

Several years ago, a husband attending a marital therapy group for the first time responded to a discussion of marital arguments by stating that he had never been angry with his wife in fifteen years of marriage. His wife said she knew he had been angry at her but that he always denied it.

A few weeks later, he manifested all of the behavioral signs of anger when his wife told about an embarrassing incident. His voice tone became louder; his words were clipped; he sat forward in his chair; his hands were clenched into fists. When his wife inquired, he denied feelings of anger. The scene fortunately had been videotaped. The man viewed the tape and became tearful. He then could see that he looked angry and must have been angry; yet, he denied having experienced any feelings of anger. This was a result of habitually discounting body awareness.

Schiff suggests that after awareness of the existence of a stimulus, the next stumbling block to problem recognition is discounting the significance of the stimulus. For example, the husband may have been aware of an angry feeling (internal stimulus) after viewing the tape but said to himself, "Everybody gets angry." Since everybody does it, the event is not seen as a problem.

If you are aware of an unpleasant stimulus and recognize its significance, you still may not be in a position to define the unpleasant event as a problem to be solved. You may recognize that a problem exists, but the problem will not be a significant one for you to solve unless you view the stimulus in question as capable of being changed. For example, farmers are certainly aware of the weather. Their livelihood depends on weather conditions. However, farmers do not spend much time trying to control the weather because of the low probability of their actions having any effect. Problems without possible solutions are not defined as significant problems (unless you want to hassle), and no effort will be expended toward dealing with the uncomfortable stimulus.

A clinical example of discounting the changeability of a situation involves a young woman who initially complained of being depressed but denied any known cause for her disphoria. "I have two wonderful children, a good husband, and a happy home. I have no reason to be depressed."

Mrs. Lane was discounting and therefore not aware of the source of her discomfort. I explained the various aspects of discounting to her. As I talked about disbelief in the probability of change being a discount, she began to weep: "My husband has no time for me. He is a sportsman and is always away from home, but I knew that when we married. He won't change and I won't leave him, so I just push it out of my mind. I know it is useless to complain about what is. It's hopeless."

In the above two examples, discounting appears to be of use in the "farmer" example and a problem-solving block in the clinical example. In fact, excluding unimportant stimuli, recognizing one's limitations, and resolving not to waste time on activities with a low probability of success are all important skills in getting through life.

The difficulty lies in the fact that the person doing the discounting may not know the difference between the two. Overcoming discounts without outside opinions or professional assistance is difficult. Good problem solvers do not hesitate to use such resources.

Finally, the problem will not be defined as solvable until you believe that you are personally capable of changing the unpleasant stimulus. For example, a man may believe that anger can be dealt with by some people. However, he may believe that because he is a redhead, he has been constitutionally destined to be angry.

Furthermore, Schiff states that it is possible that you may continually discount stimuli, related problems, and problem-solving options, and therefore you may never look for solutions. You are not getting your needs met, but you fail to recognize that the needs exist, are important, or can be met.

To summarize, successful problem recognition requires that you:

1. Be aware of stimuli—internal and external.
2. Acknowledge the significance of stimuli.
3. Maintain your belief that the situation is change-able and that you personally have the ability to change it by exercising available options to solve your problem.

Defining Problems

Problem solving will not be possible if the problem is originally conceived in such a way that a solution is un-likely. The following interview is an example of a prob-lem that was originally misidentified:

Dr.: "Tell me why you are here, Mrs. B."

Mrs. B: "Yes, Dr., I am depressed."

Dr.: "How long have you been depressed?"

Mrs. B: "About six months."

Dr.: "What happened six months ago?"

Mrs. B: "My husband had an affair. Well, he appar-ently had been having an affair for a long time, and I found out last September."

Dr.: "Tell me about the thoughts that go along with your depressed feeling."

Mrs. B: "I don't know about any thoughts, but the affair makes me depressed all the time. Things will never be the same."

If Mrs. B is unwilling to change her problem defi-nition, she is not likely to find a solution. Her husband's affair is history. If the fact that he had an affair must change to ease her depression, the problem has no solution.

Dr.: "How is the affair currently a problem to you?"

Mrs. B: "I am depressed about it."

Dr.: "Specifically, when do you think about your husband's affair?"

Mrs. B: "Why, every time he goes on a trip, Dr. You see, I worry every time he leaves that he will want another woman. I worry until he returns, and he travels at least two days each week. That's why I'm depressed."

Dr.: "Then you're depressed because you worry, in your head, about your husband's trips?"

Mrs. B: "That's right, Dr."

Mrs. B did not fully accept responsibility for her thoughts for several more interviews. In solution training, she correctly saw that her real problem was her decision to worry each time her husband left the house. Her worry was not related to his current behavior, nor could her worry affect his behavior. Whether he decided to remain faithful or to escalate his woman chasing, Mrs. B would experience the same distress.

Mrs. B originally defined her problem as: "My husband had an affair six months ago, and I am depressed about it." This conceptualizing of the problem leaves her without a solution. History won't change. Later, she identified the problem as "her own thoughts and fantasy of future events," which were directly under her control. Therefore, the problem became a solvable one.

Mrs. B eventually identified several subsets of her problem, all of which were solvable because their solutions related to changes in rules she had learned and accepted. New learning can take place, and new decisions can then be made leading to problem solutions. For example, Mrs. B falsely believed that her worry and resulting depression would have some control over her husband's behavior. Another belief, that her marriage should have been perfect, was suggested by her earlier statement, "Things will never be the same." She thought that she ought to be depressed in the face of a human error, such as an extramarital affair. So Mrs. B was faced with changing her rules about her marriage being perfect and her false belief that her worry could control her husband's behavior.

All of the problems had their solutions within her personal control. This is the key to problem defining for yourself.

Defining Problems for Others to Solve

People in authority are in a position to create and define problems for those under their direction. They can define problems that are solvable or, inefficiently, problems that have a low probability of being solved.

A client seeking counseling for depression had chosen to work at a manual labor job even though he was very bright. As a child, he had wanted to perform to impress his father. As a youngster, he was very creative and motivated to achieve. His father had hoped to stimulate his child's creativity and motivation by never appearing quite satisfied with his production. However, in this way, the father developed an unsolvable problem for his son. The son was supposed to meet his father's expectations, while the father was committed to remain unimpressed as a motivational technique. His son, never having his efforts rewarded, finally gave up trying and settled for a banal existence.

A personal example of poor parenting (setting up a problem for my children with a solution beyond their capabilities) occurred when my five-year-old twins were fighting. Their altercation was disturbing my writing, and I was the babysitter that night. They came to me, both crying and accusing each other of wrongdoing.

My strategy was one that had been successful many times with my two older sons.

"I want the two of you to go to your room. Don't come out until you have a workable plan to get along with each other for the rest of the night," I commanded.

"Sometimes you forget," my daughter pouted.

"Forget what?" I asked.

"Sometimes you forget we're only five," she explained.

I had defined a problem for which my ten- and twelve-year-old sons could find a solution. However, my five-year-old twins were not yet old enough to be efficient plan writers.

I saw my error and recovered (somewhat embarrassed) by asking her what a five-year-old could do about fighting.

She answered, "We could just stop it."

"That will be fine," I agreed.

Recently a client of mine was very distraught about her new job. Her boss would signal a problem in her work performance by giving her a dissatisfied look. He would not give her a straightforward answer when she asked whether anything was wrong. The boss was a passive individual who did not like direct confrontation. The employee would then try hard to figure out what the problem was and change her behavior in order to make her boss happy. Their unwritten supervisory contract was like a hide-and-seek game: "I'll look displeased, and you try hard to figure out what's wrong." This boss was reducing the probability of his employee solving her work-related problems by not defining the problem clearly. Of course, the employee was rewarding his behavior by accepting responsibility for figuring out the problem. The end result was inefficient problem solving.

Effective bosses, parents, teachers, and other authority figures define problems for those under their direction so that the problems have solutions. They then reward their charges for problem solving. However, it is important to remember that the same set of circumstances can be defined in different ways. Creative problem definitions lead to high-probability solutions rather than to problem-solving interference.

A Problem Can Be Defined In Many Ways

My clients, with either clinical or managerial problems, frequently fail to redefine an unworkable problem once they decide what the problem is. Any situation that produces discomfort, fails to satisfy needs, or threatens our well-being can be conceptualized from many different angles. The possible problem definitions are endless. Each definition excludes solutions pointed to only when the problem is redefined in another manner.

Gary Davis has pointed out that when an inventor defines his problem as "how to build a better mousetrap," he limits his problem-solving actions to trapping "mice." There are many other ways to rid the world of mice. Trapping is restrictive.

In a problem-solving group for first-line supervisors, a supervisor described her difficulty with a problem employee. After a discussion she defined her problem as "how to motivate an employee to get to work on time." A second but related problem was "motivating him to meet production quotas." The group brainstormed, but the supervisor was not satisfied. She had taken most of the actions suggested already and with negative results. She finally admitted that the change probability was small because management, out of fear, was not supportive of supervisory personnel. The company was involved in a lawsuit for firing an employee. Management put out the word, "Don't fire. Work it out some other way."

The supervisor later redefined her problem as "how to get support from management." She got this support. A group of supervisors and managers (along with the company attorney) worked out a means of documenting poor performance to satisfy the court that the termination of any employee was not an arbitrary action.

If the manner in which you have defined your problem does not point to a solution, redefine as many times as necessary until the definition points to action leading to a solution, that is, a reduction in the discomfort created by the problem.

Problem-Solving Exercise

If you are facing a problem that does not yield to your efforts to find a solution, the following exercise will be helpful:

1. Set up two chairs and externalize what you say to yourself. Tape record your conversation, and listen for loopholes in your definition.
2. Ask yourself, "What is the probability of solving this problem as I have defined it?" Sometimes clients will commit themselves to a course of action to solve a poorly defined problem. When asked about the probability of success, they reply zero.

They have decided to "try" to solve the problem and have stopped creatively considering problem solving. Once they face the low probability of success, they are in a position to begin again to redefine the problem so that it is solvable.

3. Think of the problem situation that is bothering you. Write as many different definitions of the problem as you can think of. For example, a client defined his problem as "getting along with a boss who resents him." Later he defined his problem as "getting to work on time," which was more under his control and pointed to a specific action.

4. Decide if your new definitions point to easier or more efficient solutions. Does your definition point to an action *you* can take?

Chapter 3

Is Somebody Else Responsible for Your Feelings?

You have clearly defined the problem. You have defined the problem so that a probable solution exists. You know what your wants and needs are. However, are you taking the responsibility to solve the problem you have defined?

The first step in being responsible is a decision about who owns the problem. If you are experiencing discomfort, then you own at least a piece of the problem and are therefore responsible for the solution. If a second person puts a problem in your lap involving his discomfort, you may want to help him get his needs met; but you don't own the problem and you don't bear responsibility to solve it. Many problems have several partners in ownership, since several people are experiencing discomfort.

The next important step if you own the problem is to take complete responsibility for *your* behavior, *your* thoughts, *your* feelings. In seeking a workable solution, the amount of responsibility you shift to sources outside of yourself will be inversely proportional to the amount of energy you put into problem solving.

For example, if you attribute 90 percent of the problem to another person, you will invest only 10 percent of the energy actually necessary for a solution. Of course, problem-solving energies are not generally quantified, but the assignment of percentages demonstrates how efforts relate to your perception of the causes of the problem.

In my practice, most of the people who consult with me are in some way or another blaming their bad feelings on somebody else or on some outside situation. Even if a person comes into my office and begins berating himself for his own inadequacies, somewhere in his conversation he will shift responsibility to other persons or situations. I don't doubt that most people could thoroughly justify what they are saying. People put a great deal of energy and creativity in justification of why they are doing whatever they happen to be doing. It may be a fact that other people have often treated you unfairly and circumstances have at times put you in awkward situations. I do not argue with the facts regarding the above view of responsibility. However, I do argue with the basic assumption that somebody else is responsible for your bad feelings.

Don't Narrow Your Options

If you are willing to stick to the argument that others are in fact responsible for your feelings, either good or bad, you immediately put yourself in a very weak position. Your only option, then, is to pressure, convince, sell, or coerce others into changing their behavior so that you won't feel bad or so that perhaps you will feel better. The odds are that the second person likes what he or she is doing or would stop it on his or her own initiative. In general, the way we handle this dilemma is by causing (whenever possible) enough pain to the other person so that we can then say, "I'll stop if you will." This procedure is seldom effective and usually ends with both people hurting, rather than solving the dilemma. It is illogical, when you consider the facts, to think that it is easier to change someone else's behavior rather than to change your own behavior or to control your own emotions.

When you are in a position of telling yourself that someone else or something else is responsible for your bad feelings and that is where you are going to focus your energy and talents, you may in fact be able to get the other person to change so that you won't feel bad. However, you are working from a very weak position. You really have only one choice—to get the other person to change. If you are willing to take responsibility for your own feelings, both good and bad, that puts you in a very strong position with many options.

Most of us at least verbalize our willingness to take responsibility for our own feelings, answering yes to the question, "Do you accept responsibility for your own feelings?" However, I discovered some years ago that such a commitment results in very little change. What I found is that we really don't know what we are agreeing to. I found that when we look at the component parts of the responsibility issue we are not as likely to accept responsibility for our feelings. While at a Miniscript workshop in Baton Rouge, Louisiana, in 1975 with Taibi Kahler, I was given a good deal of insight into how to clarify what this agreement means.

False Beliefs About Self-Responsibility

How do you define your commitment to self-responsibility? What are your reactions to the following statements?

1. Other people can make me feel bad by what they say or do, and they have a responsibility to do so under certain conditions.
2. Other people can make me feel good by what they say or do, and they have a responsibility to do so under certain conditions.
3. I can make other people feel bad by what I say or do, and I have a responsibility to do so under certain conditions.
4. I can make other people feel good by what I say or do, and I have a responsibility to do so under certain conditions.

We are taught to believe that these four statements are true, when in fact they are totally false. This idea may shock you. Once a lady actually called me a Communist for voicing such radical ideas. There is one exception: if somebody physically beats you, it will make you feel bad physically. But I'm not talking about that sort of bad feeling.

Invite vs. Make

The key word in each of the following sentences is *make*. Nobody can *make* you feel any way. The most another person can do is *invite* you to feel either good or bad. The invitations can be very strong; because of your particular place in your own personal growth, you may or may not buy into these invitations. However, they can't *make* you feel any way. You define the kind of bad feelings that you have, and you decide when you will feel bad and how long you will keep the bad feelings. If you mention in a conversation that you do not like a person's tie or a person's dress, some people may get anxious. Some people may say, "Well, thanks for the information." Others may get angry; some may get depressed. The point is that the stimulus is the same for everybody, but different people will define it differently.

No Justice

The idea that someone else can make you feel either bad or good or that you have the same control over them is neither rational nor just. Following are examples of how I view this situation.

Let's say there is an old gentleman driving down the interstate highway. He is a real stickler for driving within the speed limit and is very conservative. He minds his own business, and he always strives to do the right thing. A teenager speeds by him doing ninety miles per hour. He clutches the wheel and thinks, "Good lord, that kid endangered my life and his life. I hope they catch him and put him *under* the jail."

Such an individual is likely to go home in such an uptight condition that his ulcer will act up and he cannot eat his supper. And he will tell his wife that some kid "made him so mad" by driving fast. When you talk to such an individual who operates under the assumption that other people can make him feel a certain way, he will assume that all decent right-thinking people would get angry when they see someone breaking the law and endangering other people's lives. The natural thing is to get angry, he may think. Further, it is his responsibility to do so. To do less would be not to care.

Now had this gentleman been able to ride with other persons whom this young man passed, he would have seen many different feelings generated by the same stimulus. Some people would get angry as he had done. Some wouldn't even see the speeding car. A few might say, "Boy, I remember when I was young. It sure was fun to drive fast." Some people would get frightened and others depressed. All kinds of feelings would be generated by this one stimulus of a young man exceeding the speed limit. But our original character feels that every time "X" happens, he will have "Y" feelings. As long as he believes this, he is trapped into that situation.

Now the injustice is that this old fellow hasn't done anything wrong. He is driving the speed limit. However, he is the one who is feeling bad, and chances are that the young man is not feeling bad at all. He is going down the road somewhere feeling fine. If you are willing to upset yourself every time another makes mistakes, you are going to have long periods of being upset. Your only solution is to spend less and less time around people and their imperfections.

What about the noncaring mentioned earlier? Should you accept everything you meet in the world without feeling? Actually, the old gentleman above has the freedom to get angry if he chooses. He may even use his anger constructively as motivation to do something about reckless drivers. However, he can't logically maintain that the control of his feeling lies in the speeding car. He has the opposite choice of not getting angry. That is a particularly wise choice if he intends to do nothing about what he has witnessed.

What About Good Feelings?

About making other people feel good—what's wrong with that? Actually there is nothing wrong with giving or accepting an invitation to feel good. But another person cannot make you feel good, nor do you have any control over the good feelings of others. If you get an invitation to feel good, great! If you have an opportunity to do something nice for someone else, super! My guess is that most of you have had the experience in which people that you care about are feeling down. You set out to cheer them up and find that they are not interested in being cheered up. The problem is, if you consider that you *can* make them feel good and you have done your best and they are not cheered up, then you may end up with two people feeling bad. In this situation, you have done something nice for somebody, and you are feeling bad about it because it did not have the desired effect. It follows that you must have done something wrong if you originally assumed that you had the power (done the right way) to make them feel good.

What Happens When You Accept Responsibility for Yourself?

A lot of people say, "That is all well and good, but I get upset anyway. I can't help it, and I don't have control over myself." Actually, you could know that the above statements are false and still end up feeling bad. The important thing is to recognize where the responsibility lies. If you really believe that you are responsible for your feelings, you are in a good position to grow personally. That is, if you are feeling bad about something that has happened and you want not to feel bad the next time it occurs, it is up to you to read the books, get the experience, talk to your minister, go into therapy, or do whatever it takes to deal with those feelings. If you put the responsibility on another person or situation, you are helpless to do anything to change.

How Much Say-So Do You Have Over Your Feelings?

All of us humans have a great deal of control over our bodies and minds. The following chapters discuss specific skills in controlling bad feelings. However, you already have a great deal of say-so (which you may not be using) over your body and emotions.

One indication of body control is that one-third of the population are placebo responders. That means that they can be given a chemically inert substance, such as a sugar pill, and their bodies will do whatever they think the pill is made for. Some people might see this ability to be fooled as a weakness. Another interpretation, the one I favor, is that they are powerful people who can do a lot for themselves. They can speed up their heartrate and slow it down, they can lower their blood pressure, and they can tolerate severe pain if they are told that it is not going to hurt. That is power! In fact, most people can control their bodily functions with the proper biofeedback. Biofeedback simply tells you what your body is doing, and with that information you can learn to control the function.

We may doubt our own control over feelings because most of us have had the experience of "deciding" to feel different with no positive results. Your decision to change is important; however, changing feelings takes skill and must follow the rules of changing any learned behavior. The original decision to change will allow you to avoid uncomfortable feelings. You have the know-how to change these feelings, but in the past you may have chosen not to use it.

If you decide right now to take responsibility for your feelings and to put the best possible interpretation on events around you, about 5 to 10 percent of your bad feelings will never occur. If a friend has not called for a few weeks, you can decide that she doesn't like you any more and feel bad. Or you can put the best possible interpretation on the event by realizing that there are many other possible reasons for not calling and stay in your okay feelings.

What if that friend finally calls and tells you that she doesn't like you? You still have many options affecting your feelings. You may grieve for the loss of a friend but decide not to "kick" yourself mentally, blame yourself for the loss, or suffer unnecessarily. If you normally "get down on yourself" for one week in similar circumstances, you may decide to get over the bad feelings in two days. The point is, once you know the feelings are not totally controlled by outside circumstances—that you are responsible—you can change what you feel in some way or begin actively learning the skill to change it on the next go-around.

Yes, But . . .

A few people are so locked into their false beliefs that they reject the concept presented here. Most, after the initial shock, are enthusiastic. In this latter group, about one-half become disenchanted with the new approach when they consider the supposed implications. These individuals have one of several "yes, buts."

"Yes, but where does caring for others fit in? If you really care about somebody, shouldn't you hurt if they hurt?" The "shouldn't" doesn't really apply. The problem of "shoulds" and "oughts" will be discussed elsewhere. However, when an invitation to feel bad is initiated by someone you love, the invitation is likely to be strong. You are free to hurt if someone close to you hurts. The important factor is that you keep responsibility for the hurt in perspective. It is your hurt, and you are responsible for it as well as what to do next about it.

There is a real risk in closely attaching your feelings to those of another. I see family pathology resulting around ideas like: "I can't let my feelings show, or my wife will get depressed again." The strongest marriages are by those people who do not *need* each other to exist. People who can't live without their mate (that is, those who live to some extent within his or her "skin") are generally destructive to the relationship. Two people who decide to spend their lives together because they respect, enjoy, and love each other and still could be okay on their own have a stronger bond.

"Yes, but if you don't respond to other people's invitation to feel, won't you be cold and generally unfeeling?" No, not at all; you will just feel bad less often if you choose to. Actually you can still have feelings, both good and bad, when you choose. Both feeling states are important in getting on with living. However, when you take the freedom to be responsible and choose, you can't shift the blame to others for your problems.

You will have less fear of closeness with others when you avoid invitations to feel bad. Fear of closeness develops out of the idea that other people can hurt you. Those of you who take responsibility for yourselves are generally warm, energetic, and creative. However, some people are so frightened of their own feelings that they shut those feelings off. I am not suggesting that. Outwardly they may appear calm and unruffled, but they are in fact uptight, fearful individuals. This kind of reaction does not develop out of being responsible for your feelings. These people generally think that others can make them feel bad if they don't put a lid on their feelings.

"Yes, but aren't some bad feelings legitimate and *real?"* Grief following a loss, frustration following a failure, or fear following a near-accident are examples of real, physiological reactions to psychological stress. However, even these feelings are maintained, increased, or dealt with in a brief period of time by personal control rather than being externally determined. "Genuine" uncomfortable feelings (anger, fear, sadness) motivate you to some rational action; unhealthy feelings lead to passive complaining or irrational behavior. All feelings are "real" in the sense that they are felt. All feelings are logical in the sense that they logically agree with attitudes from which they are generated. However, the attitudes and beliefs may themselves be illogical, leading to unhealthy feelings.

"Yes, but what about conditioned emotional responses? Aren't these automatic reactions over which you have no control? Isn't there a lot of evidence that your environment controls how you behave?" It is true that you can be conditioned to fear certain situations.

Again the important factor is to keep the responsibility in perspective. If you have had an unpleasant experience in a given circumstance and you continue to feel uneasy in similar circumstances, it's your responsibility to correct the bad feelings. If you choose to feel helpless and spend your time blaming the unfortunate event, then you are stuck. It is true that learning to feel in relation to a specific stimulus follows the laws of learning and that relearning may take time. That's why "willing" not to feel a certain way doesn't always work. In the following chapter, specific techniques are discussed that counter conditioned emotional responses.

If your environment in general is inviting you to do things you don't want to do, take responsibility for changing your environment. You be the controller. You do not have to allow yourself to be controlled.

The fact is, we often act *as if* others can make us feel good or bad, and we do often accept responsibility for causing others to "feel." Such a condition is not always a problem. However, when your style of life stops working for you and you are prevented from solving a problem because *someone else is responsible for your feeling or you for theirs*, reaffirm your responsibility and solve the problem.

Responsibility vs. Blame

It is important that you not confuse *responsibility* with *blame*. Often a client has misunderstood this chapter and has concluded that he was to blame and someone else was blameless, or that his problems were his own fault. Blame is not the question here. Harry Boyd makes this same point in his statement, "Though the words 'blame' and 'responsibility' are not synonymous, many people in our culture use the terms interchangeably." He goes on to point out that we learn to confuse responsibility and blame. Thus, to avoid blame we also learn ways to avoid responsibility.

Self-Responsibility Exercise

1. Think back over the past seven days and identify those bad feelings for which you blamed other people or situations.
2. Take your responsibility as described in this chapter. Look for options in solving your problems and dealing with your feelings rather than justifying your suffering.
3. Decide to accept responsibility for your feelings and problem solve instead of blaming for the next seven days.

With this exercise, my clients (and I) have been able to give up a portion of our bad feelings with no additional skills involved other than the decision to do so. The skills you will gain in the following chapters will increase your success in combatting unnecessary bad feelings.

Chapter 4

The Past Doesn't Have to Control the Present

"Experience is the best teacher" goes the bromide. Who can argue with such obvious logic? We do learn from experience. Amazingly, however, we are capable of having experiences, time and time again, from which we fail to learn the obvious. In my therapeutic activities, in consultation with company presidents, in watching my friends, and in moments of insightful self-observation, I witness nonproductive, destructive behavior continue in spite of experience. Bright, aware individuals make the same mistakes over and over.

I remember a distraught father who asked, "Doc, I hope you have a treatment for a stupid kid. I have been beating my son's butt thirteen years for his lying, and he still does it." In this case, neither father nor son had learned from experience. The father continued what he thought "should" be the remedy in spite of the negative results, yet neither son nor father lacked intelligence or problem-solving ability in other areas. Habits persist long after the actions they produce have ceased to be effective. More than other creatures, we continue

40

outmoded behavior because at one time we made the *decision* that these actions were the "right thing to do."

Your previous experience with a situation similar to the one at hand will be the major factor in your solving the problem. Your experience will provide a psychological set, a way of thinking that has a high probability of solving your problem while excluding irrelevant information. Perhaps you have already established a habit that will lead to a solution, and your problem may be solved without your thinking about it—more or less automatically. Your experience may actually elicit a hierarchy of habits that can be systematically sampled until your problem is alleviated.

Your experience can also be the biggest hindrance to your problem solving. Old rules may lead you to the same old dead end or cause you to exclude possible solutions from consideration. Wolfgang Köhler, in a classic problem-solving experiment, observed the ape, Sultan, figure out how to fit two sticks together to retrieve a banana out of his reach. If Sultan had had a rule learned from his mother that "apes don't use sticks to solve problems," he would have never reached his banana. Human beings have many such rules: "It's not polite to . . . " "Never . . . " "You should always. . . ." Transgressing these rules would sometimes lead to new ideas and possible solutions.

A decision such as "You can't tell me anything" or "You can't make me," may exclude new learning. A decision that you must be in control in your personal relationships will lead to shutting off feeling (experienced as loss of control) and refusing to ask for help when you might save time and energy by doing so. A decision to depend on others to be responsible for solv-

ing your problems will lead to not thinking of a solution and waiting to be rescued. So your previous
experience may block problem solving, and you may
spend your energy and creativity defending the block.

An example of how a belief or mind set may block
problem solving was reported by Martin Scheerer in
Scientific American. He proposed a problem of connect-
ing nine dots (Fig. 2) without lifting the pencil or re-
tracing. Most people add to the definition from their
own past experiences, assuming they must be neat and
stay within "limits." That is, they have a psychological
set that leads them to believe they can't draw lines *be-*
yond the dots. If they follow the limits of this psychological set, the task is impossible. Breaking an old rule
and going beyond the lines will allow a solution.

When we seek psychological treatment because our
lives are not working out like we want and we are depressed, the probability is that we will devote much of
our energy and creativity to defending our current
life-styles. We justify our right to feel depressed. We
list a hundred good reasons for having our undesirable
feelings. If we win this argument, we lose!

Some of us expect our feelings to change without
having to change ourselves. We may consult with well-
meaning physicians, who, wanting to relieve our suffering, administer medication—which eliminates the
motivation to learn better problem-solving techniques.
Still others of us complain of feeling bad, but we don't
really expect our feelings to change because we think
we "ought to feel bad" due to conditions that exist. We
feel we deserve "it" and want to be "understood" in our
uncomfortable state.

I recall a critical incident in my own personal psycho-

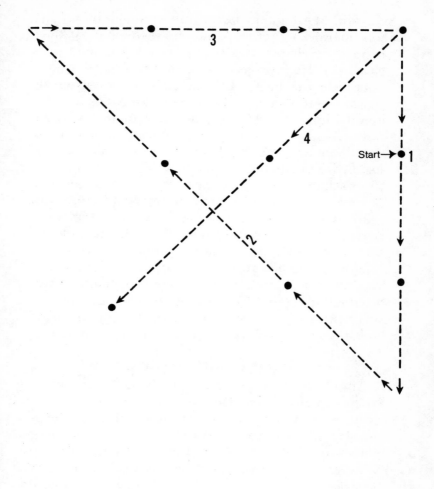

Figure 2
SOLUTION TO PROBLEM IN
"SCIENTIFIC AMERICAN"

therapy. My therapist began to focus on why my life was not working for me, and for a moment my path of productive change was clear. Then my thoughts focused on, "He is projecting his own pathology. What a poor technique he has. I have seen him work better; he must be tired. Actually, he has had no more experience as a therapist than I." I began to feel angry. "Now, the son-of-a-bitch is pushing me for a commitment that I don't want to make." Whether or not my thoughts were justified is beside the point. I had missed my opportunity to change. I had used my energy to fortify my state of being rather than to increase my personal growth.

You define your concept of reality gathered from experience. Whatever distortions you introduce determine your awareness, what you think and feel about the world, and how you behave, both verbally and nonverbally. If a problem you face has a solution and you are not finding that solution, your experiential concept of reality does not contain the right information or contains an active block to your finding the solution.

What Is the Problem?

Am I saying that we don't really change significantly? No, people do change. However, we do not change easily when conditions around us suggest a change is needed, as do servomechanisms. An air-conditioning system cools the air and shuts down, reactivating as the air warms. We persist in old behavior long after such behavior ceases to be useful and therefore fail to solve the problem. Why? What are the mechanisms for denying reality, and what are the motivations for doing so?

The reasons are multiple and complex. First of all, a

change in behavior or attitude does not take place in isolation. Changing one behavior may disrupt several other behavior-belief systems that are highly valued. Changing one belief may be incongruent with other beliefs and thus may create discomfort. Changing a significant amount is experienced as a loss of self. Therefore, new experiences are distorted, redefining reality so that change and discomfort are avoided. Another possibility is that previous experience may not have included information appropriate to solving the problem at hand, so the required change is not in our behavioral repertoire.

Mechanisms for Redefining Reality

In essence, we don't have very many new experiences. We keep ourselves from novel information by mechanisms that shape new data to fit expectations more consistent with old data. Richard Bandler and John Grinder describe three mechanisms by which we, as humans, cause our experience to differ from reality: generalization, deletion, and distortion.

Generalization

Generalization is a process in which experience with past stimuli is applied to current situations whenever the stimuli are similar to the previous situation. Without the ability to generalize, we would have to relearn how to drive a car or open a door each time we are confronted with an unfamiliar car or door. Generalization allows previous experience to have value in solving new problems. As children we observe that dogs that growl have a high probability of biting, while dogs that wag their tails have a low probability of biting.

Generalizing this early experience into the future allows us, when meeting an unfamiliar dog, to make a prediction about the animal's probable behavior. Experiences that don't generalize (usually because stimuli in a new situation are too dissimilar) are not useful learning experiences. A few years ago the original excitement about biofeedback therapy abated somewhat because the changes in blood pressure, skin temperature, and other conditions did not often generalize to the environment, once the biofeedback apparatus was removed.

Generalization is a two-edged sword, however. Just as useful habits can be generalized in new situations, outmoded, nonproductive, inappropriate, and unnecessary feelings and behaviors can persist in new situations. Much psychopathology is the result of generalization. J. R. Baugh et al. demonstrated that subjects who had had highly negative experiences with their fathers tended to *disrupt* communication when placed under stress by a male interviewer. Subjects with more positive father experiences didn't disrupt their communication under the same stressful conditions. Their attitude toward their fathers was apparently generalized to all males—specifically the male interviewer. Much psychopathology and prejudice are products of generalization.

Deletion

Bandler and Grinder defined deletion as "a process which removes portions of the original experience (the world) from full linguistic representation." That is, we select from all of the possible stimuli present only a portion to which we will attend. A second deletion may take place when we report, only in part, what we are experiencing.

In this chapter we are interested in the first kind of deletion—leaving out part of the stimuli present, which may, if perceived, aid in problem solving. For example, a man believes that he is very unlucky. His parents told him for years that he was the "unluckiest child in the family." Friends laughingly kidded him about the "black cloud" that follows him around. During any given day he deletes from his experience situations that might be labeled lucky. That is, he may run over glass in the road and not get a flat; or the police may stop the car in front of him in a speed trap. When he sums up his day, he only remembers that it rained on his traveling day. Again he feels unlucky. Should he not delete some of the total happenings of the day, he would be in a better position to reassess old information about his fate.

Deletion also has a positive effect on problem solving and therefore is a useful process. Attending to all stimuli present would be confusing. Only a small part of an event may be useful in solving a problem. Taking all of the event into consideration would be wasted effort.

Distortion

The third mechanism for redefining reality—distortion—involves either generalization or deletion or both, or entails creating something entirely new, like combining experiences into new wholes never before experienced. All creativity is a distortion of present experience. Distortion also "creates" negative experiences that do not exist in reality. A woman is sitting at home in relative safety. She is with a supportive family group, free from danger or threat. Yet her heart rate is accelerating, her palms are moist, and she talks of "feeling anxious." This woman is distorting her experience by fearful future fantasies about being killed in a car accident. This fear is her creation, not supported by present data. She herself says the idea is foolish, but the fear does not abate.

Jacqui Schiff hypothesizes three internal mechanisms that overlap somewhat with Bandler and Grinder's categories. These mechanisms, according to Schiff, are utilized by individuals to redefine or to distort reality and are as follows: discounting, grandiosity, and thinking disorders.

Discounting

Discounting is similar to deletion. Schiff defines discounting as "people minimizing or ignoring some aspect of themselves, others, or reality situations." For example, a man has made a previous decision that his needs would be best met by being dependent on someone else. He develops social skills to get others to take care of him. He avoids opportunity for growth if the growth is to proceed independently. He may experience a great deal of inconvenience in waiting on others to "do it for him or to tell him how to do it." He is likely to distort reality by minimizing any independent behavior on his part. He will always "check out" with someone else a decision that he was forced to make (nobody else was there) and ask if he did the right thing. Although the results are already observable before he asks for a second opinion, he feels the other person has helped him by telling him "it was okay to have done it."

Grandiosity

Grandiosity is defined by Schiff as one "involving an exaggeration (maximization or minimization) of some aspect of the self, others, or the situation." Grandiosity is used to motivate and justify certain behaviors, usually pathological ones. For example, a dependent person may say to another, "I will go crazy if you don't tell me what to do." An alcoholic might say, "I'm going to pull my hair out if I don't get a drink." These exaggerations of reality (the above two individuals are probably only mildly uncomfortable) help justify the maintenance of pathological symptoms. Schiff speaks of a delusional "I can't stand it" position, which justifies any irrational behavior that may follow.

Albert Ellis hypothesizes a condition similar to grandiosity, which he calls "catastrophic thinking"—irrational thoughts that motivate psychopathology. One of his followers, Ryan McMillan, defines the "I can't stand it" thoughts: "These are thoughts that a person can't tolerate a situation when, in fact, he can. Usually, these thoughts produce so much anxiety that a person can't think of solutions to problems he 'can't stand'. . . . These are thoughts that grossly exaggerate and dwell on tragedy. It can easily reach the point where all we feel is pain, and it is difficult to go on leading a normal life. For instance, 'my husband asking for a divorce is the worst thing that could happen to me,' or 'I can't go on living now that my daughter has died.'"

Thinking Disorder

Schiff's third internal mechanism for distorting reality is a thinking disorder. Thinking disorders may take one of several forms in distorting or redefining reality. Thinking involves awareness of internal and external reality, as well as labeling and organizing those perceptions. A focus on either the internal or the external to the exclusion of the other will result in faulty thinking. Feelings may escalate to the extent that rational thought plays no part in behavior.

Thinking disorders may be occurring when we get tied up in trivia by excessive concern with details. On the other hand, we may overgeneralize in answering universal questions such as "What is truth?" and discontinue useful thinking related to current problems. We may think selectively about information that is not helpful in problem solving, such as in obsessive thought. Or we may use fantasy in a way that prevents our dealing effectively with reality. Thought processes will be investigated further in Chapter 5.

Motivation for Distorting Reality

Why is distortion of reality a necessary human condition? A mass of data coming out of social psychology suggests that we must maintain consistency in what we believe about ourselves, our world, and our behavior or we suffer discomfort. This work, stimulated by Leon Festinger, suggests that the discomfort produced by incongruent ideas motivates us to utilize mechanisms (such as those suggested above) to recreate a state of congruency. Cognitive dissonance is a state of nonfitting cognitions. Dissonance creates discomfort, and the individual with two or more cognitions that don't fit is motivated to reduce the dissonance.

Jack Brehm and Arthur Cohen have presented dissonance in a more or less mathematical sense. They assume that the magnitude of the dissonance is related to the ratio of all dissonant cognitions divided by the sum of all cognitions (both dissonant and congruent). Following their suggestions, we can reduce dissonance without changing dissonant cognitions by taking into our cognitive systems a greater number of cognitive elements that are congruent.

For example, a little girl grows up with the cognitions that her mother lets her cry for a long period of time when she is wet and hungry. She may be uncomfortable physically with that situation but have no information that is dissonant in terms of how parents "should treat their children." As she grows older, she sees that parents in the neighborhood respond to their children in a nurturing manner. Very young children have a magical belief that parents are omnipotent and therefore never wrong in their behavior. Now the child may experience dissonance between the ideas that her parents don't treat her in a nurturing manner, that parents are generally nurturing, and that parents are never wrong. These dissonant elements are likely to create a good deal of discomfort. A child of this age may express some distress in the situation, such as wetting the bed or negative behavior.

Now suppose that this child one day hits upon the idea that she may be different. That is, she may be a special kind of child who is *unlovable*. This new idea would integrate previous information. That is, it may be a fact that her parents don't love her, parents in general love their children, and parents are never wrong. However, she is special and unlovable, and therefore an exception to the usual cases. Although she may not appreciate being a special, unlovable case, she will be more comfortable in terms of dissonance. This child will predictably attempt to prove on a regular basis that she is unlovable. For example, if a new child moves in the neighborhood, she is not likely to introduce herself in a friendly manner. Rather she may throw a rock at the newcomer and set up a rejection, thereby reinforcing the idea that she is unlovable. Only a day or so after beginning school, she will likely be identified by the teacher as a problem child. The teacher will then begin to look for problem behavior—and certainly find it.

In essence a primary motivation for fitting reality into our previous experience is that we experience discomfort to the degree that new information is dissonant or inconsistent with what we have before accepted as factual. In cases of excessive dissonance, discomfort can escalate to intense anxiety and panic. At this point we are likely to withdraw from new information and refuse to take in more data. A rule regarding the experiential model of reality is that we will strive to keep our model consistent internally, and we will stop or distort incoming information to maintain that consistency.

The EST trainers in a book by Luke Rhinehart put it similarly: "The mind wants agreement in order to survive. It wants confirmation of its point of view, of its decisions, of its conclusions. It wants to keep proving itself right."

Dissonance motivates the distortion of reality that is inconsistent with our experience because the cognitive elements in our experience are perceived as self. That is, to a large extent we are what we have experienced. To change large elements of this experience, that is to throw out or label as invalid previous cognitions, will be experienced as a loss of self. The degree of change relates to the degree of loss experienced. We are not likely to change a large number of cognitions in spite of a great deal of evidence because such a large change would threaten our concept of who we are.

Belief Systems and Life-Styles

What we believe about ourselves, others, and particular situations—our belief systems—consists of perceptions from our past experiences about which we formed beliefs, made decisions, and developed rules for living. The decisions and resulting rules relate to how to approach the world to get the most out of life, how to be worthwhile, and how to survive in perceived dangerous situations. All three areas overlap and mutually influence each other.

Getting the most out of life develops into a particular life-style that we *believe* will work best for us. Much misunderstanding and miscommunication take place between individuals talking from different life-styles, that is, "coming from different places." We each believe our style is the most logical, and we don't understand why the other person is "coming on like that."

Paul P. Mok has drawn on Carl Jung's four major personality styles to develop a personality theory, which he uses in business and industry. Mok's four styles are Intuitor, Thinker, Feeler, and Senser. I have changed the first and last labels to Theorist and Pragmatist to better communicate their meaning. Mok believes that we may change styles under stress, and he also discusses different style reactions during stressful conditions.

Theorists are idea people. They are seen by others as impractical, in their "ivory towers." They place value on theory and long-range planning. They will find more reward in arriving at a solution creatively than in implementing that solution. Therefore, they may be locked into ideas and not likely to test them out in reality. Theorists approach disorder with great anticipation. They enjoy putting discordant ideas into a meaningful whole.

The college campus is full of theorists. Professors, scientists, writers, and artists are in this group. In industry they function as long-range corporate planners and stimulate others with their ideas.

Theorists under stress will become even more detached and will tend to overintellectualize. They may overlook the reality of the situation that they face. They may be seen as rigid and unwilling to compromise their ideas. They place more value on the internal consistency of their ideas rather than on the practicality of the concepts.

Thinkers place "high value on logic, ideas, and systematic inquiry. That is, he finds satisfaction in identifying a problem, developing a variety of possible solutions, weighing them carefully, and testing them to see to it that the most logical systematic approach is followed." Thinkers use logical and rational thought processes and discount feelings as not related to problem solving. They are results-oriented and may be lacking in long-range vision or ideas.

Thinker occupational types include scientists, lawyers, businessmen, engineers, and technicians.

Under stress thinkers become overly cautious. When their world lacks order, they feel threatened and avoid risk taking. They strongly discount their feelings and the feelings of others. They look for rules to follow.

They want to proceed "by the numbers" in a correct and logical manner.

Feelers place "high value on human interaction. He seeks and enjoys the stimulation of contact with others and typically tries to understand and analyze his own emotions and those of others. His concern for people, his understanding of them, usually make him quite astute in 'reading between the lines' about what people say and do." The feeling person is seen as warm, wanting to please, and interested in others.

Occupations include social service workers, mental health personnel, salespersons, secretaries, and public relations specialists.

Under stress feelers escalate feeling over thinking. They believe that people cannot think clearly in the presence of strong feelings. They become impulsive and inefficient. They overreact to criticism. They may become overly dramatic and blow the situation out of proportion.

Pragmatists are action-oriented doers. They may act now and think later, sometimes causing mistakes. They are direct, practical, and get the job done. They attend to detail and ideas when these relate to getting the job done. They make things happen in an organization. They are good decision makers and hate to waste time.

Pragmatist occupations include construction workers, engineers, bankers, military personnel, physicians, production supervisors, and professional athletes.

Under stress pragmatists are aggressive and attack the opinions of others. They discount the feelings involved. They want to take action and see what happens. They may have tunnel vision and be "end" oriented, disregarding the "means." They look for quick results, often overlooking long-range consequences.

There is no "best" type. Each could be appropriate depending on the situation. Most of us have a cross section of all the styles, but we will have favorites. Mok speaks of *primary* and *back-up* styles. As good problem solvers we can implement a less-favored style when the situation calls for it. Also, we do not discount the actions of others operating from a style different from our own. We learn how to communicate with others, whatever their style.

Mok points out that the theorist "places a premium on communications which are well thought out, emphasize the central thought, principle idea, or values, and which do not waste time or space on details." Thinkers listen better to logical, organized, and systematic communications. They may omit feelings, which antagonizes feelers who want to know they are talking to a human being with feelings. They appreciate "illustrations based on real people in real situations."

Pragmatists don't appreciate being buttered up, receiving background information, or listening to verbiage. They want the facts necessary to take action. They want to maximize time in functional communication and minimize the frills.

Life-style will be discussed further in Chapter 6 in relation to its interaction with other parts of the belief system.

How to Be Worthwhile

As a child you experienced yourself as having worth in relation to your parents and other significant adults. When your parents were proud of you, you felt worthwhile. Rules about maintaining this state functioned for you as a child learning about the world, particularly the social world. They even work for short periods of time in the adult world. However, these false beliefs about worthiness are responsible for most of our unnecessary bad feelings.

Albert Ellis has written extensively about irrational beliefs related to self-worth, which cause neurotic behaviors and feelings. Taibi Kahler has a more comprehensive theory, which takes into account the behaviors that correlate with the irrational beliefs.

Kahler labels his irrational beliefs as *drivers*. He lists them as follows: Be Perfect, Hurry Up, Be Strong, Please Me, Try Hard. These five attitudes are cultural and, Kahler believes, possessed by all members of our culture. However, we each have favorites and spend much of our day in one or two of the drivers and a smaller portion of our day in the remainder. These attitudes are presented to us by our parents, the church, the school, and other cultural institutions as "how to be of worth in the world." We have been bombarded with this information over a long period of time and from so many sources that the attitudes make sense to us. We may think that the road to success is dependent only on the ability to do things perfectly, to do them fast, to be strong or put up a good front, to learn to please people, and to try hard at whatever we do. We think that such attitudes and corresponding behaviors are bound to develop the full extent of our potential.

The flaw in this belief, however, is something that we are never told in our upbringing. The fact is, none of us can continue these attitudes and their accompanying behaviors for an extended length of time. How long can we be perfect? Maybe for a few seconds, or if we are alone and not doing anything, maybe we could carry on "perfection" for a little longer. However, if we are with someone and a task has any degree of complication, perfection is impossible.

Considering another of the drivers, some of us are very skilled at pleasing others. We strive to be very sensitive to the needs of others and to deliver satisfaction whenever possible. However, if we are in a room with as many as two people, each will want different things at the same time. Again failure is inevitable.

Likewise, hurrying up has its limitations. We expend a great deal of energy going faster rather than doing or being. Those of us putting up a good front not only have a difficult time in maintaining it, but we set up a new threat for ourselves in having to worry about people seeing through this front to our feelings.

The last driver, Try Hard, seems to be the most difficult to understand. It may be that in attempting to understand we are "trying very hard" to understand. In any case, when teaching this concept, I frequently hear, "I can see how these first four attitudes get you into trouble, but you do have to try hard if you are going to be a success." Actually, those of us who try the hardest do the least. There is an inverse relationship between how hard we try and how much we do. Once we complete a task, we can no longer try hard to do it. If we put off completion, we can try hard for weeks, months, or even years. The fact is if we can prove that we are "trying hard," we may never have to do anything. Those of us who try hard are excused from "doing."

Being successful in one or more of these drivers

would be difficult enough if the conditions applied to you alone. However, if you are in a Be Perfect driver, not only must you be perfect but everyone with you must also demonstrate perfection. So your choices of failing and therefore feeling bad are multiplied by the number of people you are around. Likewise, when you are hurrying up, putting up a front, pleasing others, or trying hard, you expect the same behaviors of those people with whom you have contact; and you may feel bad if they fail to comply with the attitude.

So all the drivers apply not only to you who initiate them but also to others around you. If a person wants to please you, that person expects you to please him or her also. Ideally, when a driver is present in any of us, we want everyone else to be in that same driver. Human beings have developed, outside of awareness, a signaling to others as to their driver state. Each driver carries a constellation of observable behaviors, words and phrases, or facial expressions, which are a signal to others. It is these observables that are useful in identifying the attitude that may be interfering with your problem-solving ability. (These behaviors are discussed in Chapter 6.)

We all believe to some degree in the value of the five drivers. However, individual differences occur in the amount of time we spend in a particular driver. We have favorites that were differentially rewarded in our particular families. The order of our preferences in drivers is an important aspect of how we approach life.

Kahler has identified life patterns or *scripts* associated with the drivers. These scripts relate to the timing of success or "making it." For example, individuals who are primarily a Try Hard never get what they want most out of life. These individuals spend their lives trying hard but never making it. Another individual who is a combination of Try Hard and Please Me may have a partial success, that is, almost make it and fail at the last minute. Other individuals who are mostly Please Me experience a cyclic life. When they are pleasing others and others are pleasing them, they are on top of the world. When the pleasing stops, they get just as low as they were high.

When persons are predominantly into the Be Perfect driver as a way to make it in the world, they put off a feeling of success until everything is perfect. Of course, no matter how successful, they are never perfect, and they never enjoy their success. They can't enjoy life until—until they graduate from high school, college, graduate school; until they get married; until they have children; until they make the first million. . . .

How to Survive

Robert Goulding is one of the major writers on the influence of survival messages communicated from parent to child. Goulding calls these parent messages *second-degree impasses*. His first-degree impasse is the same as Kahler's drivers. He mentions that these first-degree impasses prevent change by setting us up to fail (our parent's instructions) and feel bad. For example, a man is not likely to learn independence if he is stuck in the impasse of having to "please" others. Therefore he is prevented from changing.

Goulding's second-degree impasse involves decisions about "don't" messages from our parents. Goulding investigates ten major don't messages: don't exist, don't feel, don't be you, don't make it, don't be close, don't be important, don't be grownup, don't be a child, don't belong, and don't be well. Goulding states that these decisions were important for us at the time they were made because of their survival quality. However, as adults and in different circumstances, we are stuck with these old survival behaviors, which are no longer functional. So early decisions about how to make our parents proud of us and how to survive by complying with parental "don'ts" may hamper successful problem solving in later life.

For example, a client of mine who complained of the inability to feel much of anything remembered a series of incidents in which she was severely punished throughout her early childhood. She was able to re-member a specific time when she had been punished for crying at about age eight. On this occasion she de-cided that she would never cry again. From that time on, she prided herself that she didn't cry even when punished. She also was "calmed down" when, as a young child, she got excited over a pleasant event.

As an adult she was very stoic but particularly con-cerned because, although she cared about her family, she felt no "love" for either her husband or her chil-dren. My client had made a conscious decision, after having received a number of conditioning experiences in which feeling was punished, to deny awareness or expression of feeling states. Her parents over time and in many different varieties of communication had told her, "Don't feel." She had accepted this instruction and had decided on her own that her survival in that par-ticular family depended on her accepting the message and deciding not to feel. In essence Goulding's second-level impasse is related to what children experience as survival issues. Children must "take care of" their parents' feelings because upsetting their parents threatens their dependent relationship.

In my own clinical experience the most frequent blocking second-degree impasse rules include: don't exist, don't feel, don't think, don't make it, don't be close, don't grow up, and among my business "workaholic" clients, don't have fun.

Some of the survival messages are not communicated in the "don't" form; for example, "You've gotta prove you're right." As an adult, it is not necessary to prove you're right in what you think, feel, or do. However, when you were three or four, the only defense in case of a difference of opinion with your parents was "proving" your right to do something. Young children put a great deal of energy into proving to their parents that they are right. As an adult this action, related to past behavior, is usually unnecessary and can be a severe block to getting things done.

Two business partners are meeting to discuss a misjudgment that resulted in a financial loss. "If you hadn't talked me into this, we would have turned a good profit. Boy, was I stupid to listen to you, John."

John answers, "Now wait just a minute. . ."

If the second partner continues to put energy into defending his decisions, an argument will ensue and time will be wasted, not to mention the potential bad feeling states each may produce for himself. However, if John doesn't believe he has to prove he is right, he can use his energy in solving the problem at hand. "Okay, Marvin, let's look at some of the ways to get out of this mess." Here justification is avoided, and problem-solving action becomes the focus.

Rules resulting in getting into trouble and receiving punishment seem to go against the "survival" notion. However, consider the following: A father, a professional man, entered my office saying, "If there is one thing I cannot tolerate, it's a liar; and I have a son who is a chronic liar." I began working with the family and found the father to be correct. His son lied and did so with a high probability of being caught. His son seemed confused. He would make a commitment to be truthful, but he later (he reported) felt compelled to "do it again." Finally, he and his father got into physical altercations following his lying.

I interviewed the father about his own history. He explained that he hated lying because his mother was a frequent liar. He remembered numerous fights when his own father caught his mother lying. As an adolescent, he took his father's role of catching his mother in lies. His own account suggested that very little communication took place between his parents unless his mother messed up in some way (for example, hiding bills and saying she had paid them). My guess was that somehow this father had communicated to his son that he needed to catch someone lying in his family.

The son talked about how his father seemed to be most energized and excited after catching his son lying. His perception was that he was keeping his father interested in him by lying. This kind of communication between parents and children is behavioral and not verbal. When this teenager realized he was lying to meet his father's needs, he became angry and later made his first real commitment to stop lying (or, he added, at least not get caught). For my six-month follow-up he maintained this commitment.

Trigger Phrases

Rules in our belief systems are mediated into behaviors by *trigger phrases*. Trigger phrases are verbal labels that describe a stimulus situation or ourselves or others in relation to a stimulus situation. When the situation fits one of our phrases, we stop thinking and begin a series of automatic thoughts, feelings, and behaviors chained together and leading to a specific outcome related to a rule or belief. These behaviors and their resultants interfere with problem solving. For example, a woman has an early experience of her parents dominating her and forcing her to live life to meet their needs, disregarding her needs. She decided that she was treated unfairly and that survival in her family situation depended upon her being sensitive to "unfairness" and rebelling against the unfair situation. "It's not fair" becomes a trigger phrase for her. The thought "it's not fair" is followed by anger, verbalizing about unfairness, retaliatory behavior, withdrawal, and depression. Her behavior following the phrase will be highly predictable and is maladaptive to her current problem solving.

A clinical example of a counterproductive rule and the resulting trigger phrases was Evaline, an intelligent young woman. As a girl, she was an achiever in academics, sports, music, and extracurricular activities; and her parents expected excellent performance. However, she was the only female child in her family with several brothers. Time and time again she witnessed her parents criticizing her brothers and comparing their nonachievement with her own achievements. Deciding that she would achieve in a diminished form to "protect" her brothers and avoid guilt, she formulated a rule: "Be successful, but don't accept full credit, and don't enjoy success."

Becoming aware of the rule and making decisions to change are not enough to effect the change. *Trigger phrases that maintain the rule must be identified and confronted on a minute-to-minute basis.*

Evaline had several thoughts (trigger phrases) that she maintained (out of awareness) as a damper on her success. Praise for good performance would be followed by an unvoiced statement: "You don't deserve it" or "It doesn't really count because you didn't perform perfectly." At other times she stalemated herself or avoided an opportunity with the phrase: "You don't really have the power or energy to do it" or "It's not worth your effort because even if you do get it, you won't be happy with it."

On one occasion, after Evaline received an excellent job promotion, she expressed her thoughts: "It really doesn't feel right. I mean, I wanted it a few months ago. I guess it came too late; it felt anticlimactic."

My client recalled a teacher asking her, "How do you avoid being conceited about all your accomplishments?" Evaline's reply was that she imagined a smaller person standing directly in front of her who absorbed all the compliments and accolades. Evaline felt proud for that other smaller person, but she did not directly associate with her own success.

All the bases were covered. Evaline supported her rule about not accepting success with several drivers. She continued Trying Hard to Please others by Being Perfect and performing swiftly (Hurry Up), all the while covering up her feelings (Be Strong). Of course, all of these driver actions resulted in frequent failure and the corresponding "feeling not okay." A predictable chain reaction followed each of the above trigger phrases. Evaline would get angry and then entertain a second trigger phrase, "It's not fair" (that I do well and don't feel successful). Her anger would intensify, and in time a depression would generally follow.

The treatment intervention included setting up a chain of reactions to follow each trigger phrase that would compete with the undesirable sequence outlined above. First, she developed awareness of the trigger phrases and set up a record of the content and number of occurrences (she averaged six per day). The second step was to follow each phrase with self-nurturing. (See Chapter 10 for more on self-nurturing.) The self-nurturing was extremely important in shifting the emphasis away from pleasing other people to pleasing herself. Third, Evaline was to have an unabated fantasy of success. The fourth and final step was to choose a reward to give herself from a prepared list of such rewards. In time the trigger phrases themselves lessened in frequency, as did their associated behaviors and feelings.

A second approach to trigger phrases is to analyze each one for deleted information. For example, a client complained that he was discouraged about his wife at a time when his wife had made some positive changes. He was getting more depressed "for no reason." I asked him to remember what thought went through his mind preceding his down feeling. He wasn't sure. I then instructed him to "get into his depressed feeling" and tell me what he thought about. He reported the phrase,

"No matter what I do, nothing is going to turn out right."

I asked Mr. Martin to tell me more about that "what I do" section of the phrase; that is, what in fact had he done? He reported that he had done nothing; that is, he had not carried out any problem-solving actions. Why? Mr. Martin reported that he had done nothing because he went over all the possible actions in his mind and discarded each one. He was looking for the "one right action" without testing out some of the possible actions. For example, he believed that there was a perfect way to approach his wife about sexual matters but that he had not thought of it. He was in the passive position of doing nothing about his problem.

Next I asked Mr. Martin to define the "nothing" that was going to turn out right; that is, what situations was he considering as not changing for his benefit. He identified his sex life, job satisfaction, and personal weight loss. He had identified specific problem areas to deal with directly.

Last, I asked Mr. Martin to tell me what he meant by "turn out right"; that is, what were his criteria for success? Mr. Martin blocked himself from "making it" in two main ways. He either left the solution dependent on someone else's behavior or demanded perfection in his own behavior immediately rather than progressing in small steps toward a goal. "My wife will be turned off by my approach," he explained. "She won't understand what I really mean. As far as work goes, I can come up with creative ideas to improve my efficiency, but nobody watches. I am a much better supervisor than last year, but so what—nobody cares. The diet will be okay for a few days, and then I'll blow it. Once I eat between meals I know it's all over. Dieting is hopeless." Mr. Martin managed to measure all of his actions in such a way that they came out a failure.

What behavior did Mr. Martin's self-statement trigger? Following the thought, "No matter what I do, nothing is going to turn out right," he would experience sadness, a loss of hope. The feeling experience would be followed by one of three passive actions: he would overeat, masturbate, or do nothing (except worry). Following one of the above three, he would mentally kick himself for his nonproductive and perhaps self-destructive behavior. The anger at himself would turn his sadness into depression.

Further discussion revealed that Mr. Martin had two survival rules that he had learned from his mother: "never be successful" and "don't think" when a problem arises. He was rewarded by making mistakes and therefore forcing other people to think for him because his parents (particularly his mother) were turned on by the chance to rescue him and do things for him.

Mr. Martin was instructed to break the sequence of trigger statements, passive behavior, self-putdown, depression by using the statement, "No matter what I do, nothing is going to turn out right," as a stimulus to new and incompatible behaviors. Immediately after the phrase Mr. Martin would pat himself on the back, recognize his strengths, and focus on his positive actions during the past few days. Second, he would give himself permission to think clearly about his problem. Third, he would write down a plan of problem-solving action, take the action, and evaluate the results. The last step was to reward himself for following this new behavior pattern.

The sequence of the treatment strategy begins with recognizing that we distort reality by one of the mechanisms discussed earlier in this chapter. This is a clue that we are defending some rule or belief generalized from the past. The next step is to identify the rule itself and make a clear commitment to change the rule. The final step is to discover the trigger phrases that maintain the rule and develop an alternative set of thoughts, behaviors, and feelings that are incompatible with those nonadaptive thoughts, feelings, and behaviors associated with the trigger phrase.

Conditioned Responses Out of Our Awareness

Gregory Razran reviews experiments that suggest how previous experience can affect our current feelings, thoughts, and behaviors without our awareness. He reports on a number of studies in which internal mucosa of both animals and humans were stimulated and these in turn stimulated outward behaviors. External stimuli, including spoken words, were shown to create an internal reaction that could initiate behavior. Razran essentially gives experimental evidence to support the learning theorist Clark Hull's hypothesis that human beings develop internal implicit responses to external stimuli and that further these responses have stimulus characteristics that motivate or initiate behavior.

Razran reports the following example: "Experi-

menter noted that when his subjects were told to inhale, they manifested clear-cut plethysmographic arm
vasoconstriction in addition to changes in their pneu-
mograms. . . . The particular vasoconstriction is apparently a viscero-visceral vaso-motor reflex evoked by
respiration. Now, the experimenter told his subjects *not*
[italics mine] to inhale when the word 'inhale' was given.
But . . . the vasoconstriction persisted despite the entirely regular pneumogram—it was, presumably, 'naturally' conditioned to the word inhale and was not de-
conditioned—or inhibited—by the instruction not to
inhale when the word 'inhale' is uttered."

Razran shows that language, when used as a stimulus, is more than a simple signal in that meaning can
become a conditioned response itself. For example a
thirteen-year-old Russian boy was conditioned to se-
crete a considerable amount of saliva when the Russian
word meaning "well" or "good" was pronounced and
to differentiate from it the sound of the word meaning
"poorly" or "badly." That is, he would inhibit salivation
to the Russian word that has a negative connotation.
Later the boy was read a series of sentences that did
not contain the Russian words previously conditioned
but that carried a similar meaning. For example, the
sentence "the pupil studies excellently" produced salivation, whereas the sentence "the pupil was fresh to a
teacher" inhibited salivation. That is, the Russian boy
was not only conditioned to a particular word, but he
developed an attitude of approval or disapproval that
affected his salivation. Sentences that evoked the attitude of approval increased salivation, and sentences
that evoked the attitude of disapproval inhibited salivation.

In working with clients I have found that a particular stimulus can set off a chain of feelings, thoughts, and behaviors, each of which becomes a stimulus for the next operation in the chain until the final behavior terminates the sequence. The following example is a chain of events (reconstructed by a client in fantasy) that led to his picking a fight with his wife for "no particular known reason" and after he had made a commitment to stop fighting with his wife.

Joe was driving home, listening to the radio. An old song was playing. The song was popular one year ago when his wife had planned to leave him. Many of their arguments had occurred in the car going to and from work and as they played a tape containing the song. Now as he listened to the words and the music again, the memory of her rejection returned, followed by a "down" feeling of pressure in his chest. The idea entered his mind that she might be thinking of leaving him again. He had no evidence, but it was summer (the time it had occurred before) and she seemed more restless in the summer. "I can't stand to go through that again" was the thought followed by a pain in his stomach and chest area. He remembered her saying she felt tied down and had never had a chance to date much (they had married in high school). This thought was followed by a flash of a mental picture of her smiling at another man, followed by a "dead feeling" inside. As Joe pulled into the driveway, he felt generally depressed. He hit on the trigger phrase, "I'm being made a fool of." He went into the house and "picked a fight" with his wife.

Summary

Our previous experience leads to a concept of how we see the world. This concept is made up of conditioned responses (some of which are out of our awareness), attitudes, beliefs, decisions, rules, and ideas of ourselves in relation to others and particular situations in the world. Our experience has led to the development of a number of different habits that aid us in solving problems or that hinder problem solving when new conditions occur or when old decisions and habit responses prove ineffective in current situations. Changing long-time habits is a slow and difficult procedure, since we have many built-in mechanisms that maintain a consistency in the integration of our past experience. The resulting habits are learned, however, and therefore can be altered through new learning processes.

Chapter 5

What's Going On? Awareness of Your Feelings and Thoughts

Awareness of "what's going on" both internally and externally is essential to identifying problems and carrying out behaviors leading to solutions. Deficiencies in either external or internal awareness will delay or prevent problem solving.

As pointed out in the previous chapter, awareness involves more than processing information from the senses. That information which is allowed to be translated from sensory stimulation into cognition is greatly affected by previous experience. We tend to exclude information inconsistent with what we believe; and we accept and perhaps exaggerate information consistent with our belief system.

External Awareness

External awareness (sensory awareness) involves recognition of environmental stimuli. As good problem solvers we increase our ability to recognize external events without clouding these events by previous experiences and expectations. Our awareness is actually an interaction between our internal experience and the external perception of what is. Separating the two "realities" gives us perspective in defining the problem.

In identifying problem situations we may write down what we are aware of and confine ourselves to listing those events that can be photographed or tape-recorded. This kind of description excludes distortions through personal expectations. For example, Mr. Rustin is having difficulty in his job. He explains to his counselor that his boss is angry and does not like him. The counselor, being aware of Mr. Rustin's previous experience and difficulty with authority figures, asks him to describe exactly what's going on in his work environment. Mr. Rustin responds with interpretations rather than descriptions. He sees his boss as being "angry at him." When Mr. Rustin is encouraged to describe what might be videotaped, he states that his boss never smiles. He describes a rather serious look, which may have a number of different meanings other than his boss being angry with him. In this specific instance, Mr. Rustin was in a job situation in which the boss never smiled at anyone and was very serious and probably a mildly depressed man himself. Mr. Rustin did not in fact have a problem with his boss being angry, and therefore he could exercise his creative problem solving in areas that were real problems to him.

A good problem solver is capable of recognizing facial expressions and figuring ways to check out their meaning for that particular individual. A very straight way of checking out their meaning is simply to ask the person about his or her facial expression; for example, "Are you angry?"

A good way to train ourselves to be aware of both internal and external events is a Gestalt exercise for getting into the here and now. In this exercise we avoid getting into the memories of past events or expectations of the future (past experience) by reporting on our second by second experience (here and now experience). Many times we are spending much of our awareness, and therefore missing what is happening, by fantasizing what we expect to happen in the future or by worrying and hassling about past events. Getting in touch with here and now experience helps us identify problems and also increases our ability to appreciate what is currently occurring. Take the time to watch the sunset or look closely at a budding rose, appreciating its fragrance, texture, and color.

Feelings

Internal awareness involves recognition of thoughts or bodily experience—feelings that result from an interaction between previous experience related to the current environmental situation and the stimulus situation.

Feelings vs. Thought

Feeling is the most primitive internal awareness. All feelings are bodily experiences. If we identify a feeling purely as a thought, then we are describing thinking rather than feeling. Unless we are trained to do so, most of us from time to time confuse thoughts and feelings.

For example, you might say, "I feel like I should be doing something about my problems." Here you are not describing your feeling; you are describing a thought process of what you should do. However, there may be an accompanying feeling that you may not be fully aware of. You may be experiencing anxiety at not knowing what to do about your problem. Or you may be experiencing anger because someone else is preventing you from exercising problem-solving behaviors to get your needs met. An important therapeutic intervention is to train clients to distinguish between thoughts and feelings. Ask yourself right now as you sit reading this chapter what you are feeling; that is, what are your bodily experiences (not what is in your head).

A group therapy exercise involves going from one person to the next, asking each to state what he or she is thinking and feeling. Most individuals are able to express their thoughts. However, feelings are often confused. An individual very much in touch with what he or she is feeling might respond as follows: "Gee, when you called on me first my heart started speeding up. Now I feel myself calming down a little bit. Hey, a little tingly thing just went up and down my leg. I'm hungry. I didn't eat breakfast this morning. And I feel a kind of a warm feeling down in my stomach as I begin to relax."

When you ask people who are less aware to report on their feelings, the answer may be, "I'm feeling okay." When you request more information, they are likely to say, "I don't know what you mean. I feel all right." If you ask exactly where in their bodies they feel the "all rightness," they will likely answer, "All over, I guess." These individuals have a vague awareness of their bodies and no differentiation of the many feeling messages that they are getting on a minute-to-minute basis.

They are excluding important information that can help them be good problem solvers.

The Role of Feelings in Solving Problems

Feelings are important for their survival value. Feelings may reinforce correct behavior and thereby help us learn useful habits in problem solving. Or feelings of the more uncomfortable variety can motivate us to initiate problem solving. Two psychotherapists, Jean Maxwell and William Falzett offer the following useful information regarding feelings: "[Another] assumption is that there are no 'bad feelings'. Feelings are either comfortable or uncomfortable and are dealt with in a healthy or unhealthy fashion in the here and now. They are, therefore, healthy signs of the dynamism of human beings."

The two authors go on to describe "normal" healthy feelings. *Fear* is a loss or absence of problem-solving structure. *Anger* is defined as a response to not getting wants or needs met. *Sadness* is described as a loss of a person, thing, or relationship (either a real loss or a fantasy) and a sign of disinvestment or giving up. *Excitement* is defined as anticipation. That is, something is going to happen that is experienced as good. *Joy* or *happiness* is described as "I got what I wanted or needed." The comfortable feelings maintain or reinforce a behavior, whereas the uncomfortable feelings motivate problem solving.

The psychotherapist is most often confronted with negative affects, such as anger, fear, sadness, or guilt. Guilt is actually both a thought and a feeling. The thoughts center around the violation of our rules of what "should be." Guilt feelings are often described as a mixture of feelings. We may be angry at ourselves for violating a rule, and we may feel a sense of sadness involving the loss of a sense of the self who would not violate the rule.

The major mechanism for identifying healthy feelings is to decide whether the feelings are motivating problem-solving behaviors. Uncomfortable feelings that do not motivate some action are considered unhealthy because they contribute nothing to the individual. These unhealthy feelings are called *racket feelings* by transactional analysts. A racket feeling is defined by the following: (1) an uncomfortable feeling, (2) a stereo-type reaction to stress, and (3) a feeling leading to no appropriate action. A racket or unhealthy feeling is likely to be our most frequent uncomfortable feeling when we feel stressed. It is likely to be a feeling that interferes with (rather than enhances) problem solving.

How do we acquire these feelings, which have no biological importance for survival? Unhealthy feelings may be acquired through modeling. A girl, observing that her father or mother always gets angry when distressed, may assume that anger is an appropriate reaction to stress even if the anger does not lead to a problem solution. In another family, a boy may observe that his parents are guilty under stressful conditions, and he may assume that he ought to feel guilty when things are not working for him.

A second reason for learning unhealthy feelings is that the experience and the expression of these feelings are reinforced or rewarded by significant people during the formative years. For example, in my family, I learned to feel guilty when I had done something wrong. This behavior was reinforced by my parents. If, for example, I had acted in a very "grown-up" manner at age nine or ten by stating without guilt feelings to my parents, "Yes, I know what I did is wrong, and I am willing to accept the consequences," my parents would have been most distressed. That is, they felt that a necessary quality of their discipline was a show of expression of "feeling bad and guilty about what I had done." If I accepted the consequences with no show of guilt, the punishment would escalate. On the other hand, if I showed an excessive amount of guilt, I might get no punishment at all and be told, "Don't feel so bad about what you did. It will be okay." In this way guilt was reinforced by shortening my degree of punishment when guilt was expressed. The expression of guilt was not a conscious, deliberate act to avoid punishment on my part; I really "felt" the guilt.

A third way that unhealthy feelings are learned involves substitute feelings. For example, if anger is not permitted in a family, an individual may learn to substitute another feeling in situations that ordinarily would produce anger. Persons with such upbringing might say when someone is aggressive toward them, "I get so sad when you say mean things to me." Here individuals have substituted sadness for anger, and they will insist that they have never experienced an angry feeling.

In any case, whatever our racket feelings may be, we are likely to set up our environment so that we will have opportunities to experience our bad feeling frequently. And when invited to change the feeling into some problem-solving action, we will probably justify the feeling rather than decide to change it. We do this not because we particularly like to feel bad, but because our past experience has in some way taught us that this feeling is "right."

In a 1973 transactional analysis workshop by Curtis Steele and Nancy Porter in Jackson, Mississippi, the following justifications or "cop-outs" were suggested:

1. *My characteristics are genetic.* Here we state, for example, that we are a Taurus and "all Tauruses are stoic." Or we might say, "Sure I get angry. But I'm redheaded, and you know all redheads get angry." Some genetic reason is given to justify the feeling to avoid the necessity for change.

2. *Other people are responsible for the way I feel.* Since other individuals make me feel what I feel, they should change and not me. (This concept has been thoroughly discussed in Chapter 3.)

3. *My unconscious controls my feelings.* This is similar to the Flip Wilson statement, "The devil made me do it." We may attribute both our negative and positive feelings and behaviors to unconscious motivations. This is simply a way to avoid responsibility for what we are doing, thereby avoiding change.

4. *My bad feelings are too valuable to give up.* Here we assume that some activity must require a bad feeling as motivation on a regular basis. For example: "If I give up my sadness, my poetry will have no depth." It is true that negative aspects can be motivational. However, if we assume that creativity or productive behavior cannot occur unless we first experience a bad feeling, we are overlooking many other possible motivations.

Negative feelings are not always experienced as wholly unpleasant. Some have pleasant properties mixed with the negative. We speak of "sweet sadness" associated with nostalgia. On a television interview, the actor Walter Matthau was asked about his compulsive gambling. Matthau appeared to be very insightful; he realized that losing large sums of money was more valuable to him than winning. Matthau revealed that as a young child, he seldom knew whether his mother would be home or if he would be fed that evening. As a result, he experienced a sense of helplessness. As an adult, the feeling that most closely approximates this old familiar feeling of helplessness occurs when Matthau loses a large bet on a very close athletic contest. The feeling is intensified if he loses at the last moment of the game. The resulting negative effect has some positive aspects about it: he recalls nostalgic memories of his early childhood experience with his mother.

Exercise: Kicking the *Racket* Habit

1. Identify your most frequent uncomfortable feeling when under stress or pressure.
   a. Assume that you were at least partially responsible or cooperative in setting up the stress or pressure.
   b. List as many ways as possible that you could have set up the situation differently. Use your imagination if the logic of how you did it escapes you.
2. Can you do anything about the situation or feeling to reduce the discomfort?
   a. If the answer is yes, take action using the feeling as a healthy motivation.

    b. If the answer is no, give up the racket feeling.

    c. If you won't give it up, at least label the feeling as a racket, and don't justify or use cop-outs. If you stop fooling yourself, you are more likely to take action at another time.

  3. After you have acted to solve the problem, reward yourself with a pleasant fantasy.

An example of the handling of a racket feeling comes from my own experience. My current racket feeling is anger. Some time ago a rock broke the windshield of my car. I waited several months to get it fixed. The once-small crack grew longer and longer until I finally took the car to be repaired. The very next day I was driving behind a gravel truck and watched helplessly as three good-sized gravel rocks homed in on my new windshield. All three hit their mark, and each made a penny-sized break.

My first reaction was anger. I have no doubt that I could have justified my anger to any of my friends in light of the circumstances. I thought of a possible action. I could have turned in a license number to the police, but this usually produces no results. I could have dragged the driver out and fought; however, I knew I would not take that action. So I decided to give up my anger, and did. I was able to give up the anger because I had decided to and I had been gradually decreasing my "angers" over a period of time. And most important, I had identified the feeling as a racket feeling of no use to me. Once I successfully gave up the anger and began to calm down, I allowed myself a very pleasant fantasy and no longer felt the unnecessary anger.

Suffering

Giving suffering a separate category as a feeling may seem unusual. Suffering usually is a combination of feelings. Sadness, guilt, and anger are frequently associated with suffering. Often the sufferer's facial expression resembles that of a person in physical pain. Sufferers have learned habits to make themselves "hurt" under certain conditions.

For example, a client of mine was taught to suffer when he displeased authority. He would go to his room and "whimper" for long periods of time. Before his suffering he remembered that his father's expression would be stern. After a suffering period his father would smile and behave in an "accepting manner." An exception to the change in his father's attitude would be when "he had not suffered long enough." This experience occurred a few times, helping my client get his timing down to suit his father.

For a time I thought that disappointing an authority figure would be the only stimulus for current suffering states. This stimulus initiation was only part of the problem. He would regularly set up situations to suffer about, not necessarily related to authority. His suffering on these occasions, as well as with authority, was followed (and reinforced) by forgiveness or concern of significant people around him.

The suffering habit in this particular client lasted after he had become an otherwise "good problem solver." The remedy was quick, once he identified suffering as a problem to be solved. He first made a list (during a one-week period) of all the behaviors (of his own) that resulted in suffering. He made a plan to change each behavior to avoid suffering. Suffering was identified as a stimulus to initiate problem solving instead of supporting the suffering.

Thinking

Thinking is that process by which we recall elements of our past experience to aid us in decision making. Directing our thinking to future fantasies, we can even check out the probability of success for a possible decision that we are considering. We may, in our thinking, combine ideas from our experience that have never before been combined, thereby creating something entirely new.

Nonproductive and Productive Thinking

You may describe your problem as "thinking too much." This statement generally means that you are obsessed with or worrying about a problem rather than producing viable alternatives leading to a solution. Being obsessed or worrying is never a problem-solving type of thought procedure.

Worriers carry on their nonproductive activity because they have learned to do so. Worriers may be engaging in magical thinking, believing that their worrying may have some effect on the problem. Mothers, while worrying about their children being out late at night, may have a fantasy that their worrying itself may keep their children safe from harm. In other cases worry equals love in the minds of many. If you love someone you "worry about them."

Worry may be used to control others. "I worry about you when you're out late." The implied command here is to feel guilty about mother worrying or to stay home. "Worry" expressed often means, "I don't want you to do that anymore." It is not simply a report of a thinking experience.

People who worry actually structure their lives so that they have a particular time for worrying. This may be done by postponing a decision, gathering material to worry about, or approaching a problem by worrying rather than doing something about it.

A second kind of thinking—one that is much more productive—involves the generation of alternative actions in the face of a problem situation. These actions are checked out either in fantasy or in the real situation to judge their probable solution qualities. This kind of thinking is improved with learning. After we have additional experience, we are able to exclude alternatives that have a low probability, in our experience, of being productive. The elimination of low-probability alternatives increases efficiency and avoids time wasting.

In comparison, one type of computer program designed to problem solve operates in a similar manner. This is called a heuristic program. These programs simulate human thought in selectively pursuing goal paths that appear to be productive. Note, however, that this computer program may fail to reach the proper solution because of premature elimination of some alternatives that would lead to the desired conclusion. An important reason to examine the logic underlying computer programs is that they are designed to operate in the same way as the most productive workings of the human mind.

A similar mistake can be made in human thinking.

As hypothesized by Irving Maltzman, "thinking in general and problem solving in particular thus may involve the selection of habit family hierarchies as well as selection of specific response sequences within a hierarchy." Maltzman is saying that through our experience we develop particular families of habits that have a probability of producing the desired results. However, as with computer programs, this type of thinking may cause mistakes. Because of our experience we may limit the possibilities that we are willing to consider. A good example as quoted by Gary Davis earlier is that, if we define our task as "how to build a better mousetrap," we immediately narrow our options to trapping mice. However, if we focus on the end rather than the means and define our task as getting rid of mice, there is much more allowance for creative thinking other than trapping.

Computer technologists have developed a second kind of problem-solving program labeled algorithmic. This program is set up to house and examine all possible combinations of solution behaviors in a predetermined order. This program will check out each possibility until it finally locates the correct alternative, terminating the search at that point. The algorithmic program allows very few mistakes because it has the capacity to examine all the possibilies that have been fed into it. Human beings do not naturally have a similar thinking process. That is, very few of us sit down to problem solve by following an illogical sequence of examining every possibility within our repertoire; we only consider those possibilities perceived to be related to the problem.

Brainstorming

A derived and developed human thinking capacity that approaches the algorithmic program (although somewhat dissimilar) is the exercise of *brainstorming* or creative thinking. In brainstorming, possible solutions are considered that would be excluded in normal thinking because the alternatives seem illogical (from past experience).

Brainstorming is an exercise in which any idea that comes to mind is stated and written down without immediate judgment. That is, the judgment is saved for a later sorting; ideas are then labeled as relevant and useful or irrelevant and not useful. Alex Osborn outlined some rules for brainstorming as follows:

1. Criticism is ruled out.
2. Freewheeling is welcomed. The wilder the idea the better; it is easier to tame down than to think up.
3. Quantity is wanted. The greater the number of ideas, the greater the likelihood of a useful idea.
4. Combination and improvement are desirable. Look for how ideas can be turned into better ideas or how two or more ideas can be joined into another idea.

Osborn (as quoted in Gary Davis) lists a number of stimulating questions designed to invite creative feeling, including the following:

1. *Put to other uses?* New ways to use as is? Other uses if modified?
2. *Adapt. What else is like this?* What other ideas does

this suggest? Does the past offer parallel? What could I copy? Whom could I emulate?

3. *Modify. New twist?* Changing meaning, color, emotion, sound, odor, form, shape? Other changes?

4. *Magnify?* What to add? More time? Greater frequency? Stronger? Higher? Longer? Thicker? Extra value? Plus ingredient? Duplicate? Multiply? Exaggerate?

5. *Minify?* What to subtract? Smaller? Condense? Miniature? Lower? Slower? Lighter? Omit? Streamline? Split up? Understate?

6. *Substitute?* Who else instead? What else instead? Other ingredient? Other material? Other process? Other power? Other place? Other approach? Other tone of voice?

7. *Rearrange?* Interchange components? Other pattern? Other layout? Other sequence? Transpose cause and effect? Change place? Change schedule?

8. *Reverse?* Transpose positive and negative? How about opposites? Turn it backward? Turn it upside down? Reverse roles? Change shoes? Turn tables? Turn the other cheek?

9. *Combine?* How about a blend? An alloy, an assortment, an ensemble, combine units? Combine purpose? Combine appeals? Combine ideas?

When we are stumped in generating new ideas, creative thinking is invaluable. However, in my consultation I have found that getting individuals to delay self-criticism of their thinking, to be illogical, is difficult. We have all been overtrained to be logical. Our problem-solving models (parents, teachers, bosses) are all both critical and logical when confronting a problem.

Synectics

We can break the habit of being logical by the use of analogical thinking. A structured procedure using analogies is *synectics*. G. M. Prince indicates: "While synectics encourages flexibility and departure from usual patterns of thought, the process does contain a series of steps to serve as guides, as the leader and group desire."

The structure of synectics begins with stating the problem and developing goals, which, when reached, will be solutions to the problem. After all the logical solutions are exhausted, creative thinkers are encouraged to shift their focus from the original problem (for which they have already expressed their ideas) and to seek their goals through analogies from other "worlds of . . . "

For example, when a management group has defined the problem as absenteeism and one goal toward a solution is to develop peer pressure to come to work, the leader guides the group away from the problem by asking, "Give me an example of peer pressure from the world of animals." "The pack, you know, like a wolf pack," answers one manager. "Symbiosis, like the shark and the sucker fish or the bird and the rhino," answers another. The analogical examples of peer pressure may not have anything to do with industrial absenteeism. However, the creative thinker is now out of the rut of logical thought and is in a position to generate new ideas that may eventually lead to a solution to absenteeism.

A second synectics activity is to think of a two-word book title that captures the essences of the problem or goal and contains a paradox, such as *Responsible Dependency, Solid Softness, Consistent Variation*, or *Calm Arousal*. A book title in creative thinking helps the problem solver generalize about the problem area. This symbolic analogy "provides an extra mechanism to take a more effective vacation from the problem." Hard-core realists are encouraged to deviate from logic by the book title procedure.

A third technique is personal analogy. The problem solver "becomes" an element of the problem to be solved or the solution and, in empathy, role plays that element. "The mechanism of analogy capitalizes on the personal uniqueness of each member of the group, and the usually conflicting emotions that come help to supply the paradox sought in the Book Title. In addition, Personal Analogy can help loosen individuals and cohere a team of problem solvers. To become a hatchet or a virus is mentally loosening and broadening."

The trainer will lead the creative thinker through a series of examinations of analogies from the world of, book titles, and personal analogies. Then the group must take the metaphorical productions and apply them to the original problem. In synectics groups this step is called *force fit*: "in spite of its seeming irrelevance to the problem, force it to be useful."

When trainees balk at freeing up their thinking to an illogical extent, I have found two exercises to be helpful. First, we are not likely to take risks unless our need for strokes or recognition is satisfied. Therefore, I ask the creative thinkers to begin by bragging on themselves, to state before the group what they most appreciate about themselves. Next I and others (if this is a group exercise) give positive regard related to elements of the brag we appreciate or other facts we know about the person.

Second, I get the creative thinkers to rhyme. For example, I give the word "silly." The next person says, nilly, then willy, dilly, and so on. Generally laughter occurs. This exercise gets participants into their "childlike" thinking, which is more productive in creative thinking. The thinking exercises are usually childlike and fun.

Creative Thinking to Solve Problems

The following is a clinical example of creative thinking. Mrs. C was very depressed at the beginning of the therapy session. She refused to think of alternative actions to deal with her depression (which was partially due to self-put-downs for not being perfect). Mrs. C was very resistant to my suggestion that she brainstorm with a goal of developing new alternatives. However, she later agreed to participate and did so half-heartedly in the beginning. Later she got into the spirit of creative thinking, smiled as she generated ideas, and finally laughed. Her thinking got wild, and we both had fun.

Here are some of her creative ideas for the goal of doing something other than being depressed:
1. Take up tennis.
2. Take up with the tennis instructor.
3. Put funny notes in my husband's pockets for him to find during the day.
4. Paint my husband's face while he sleeps.

5. Work on my timing so that when a young man working in my office stretches (as I often see him doing) I will be in a position for his hand to caress my breast.
6. Develop a new sexual fantasy.
7. Buy a vibrator.

At the end of her brainstorming she was no longer feeling depressed. I asked her to look over her ideas (which were written on a blackboard) and think of a book title that would capture the essence of her creative productions using a paradox. She answered, "Turned-On Frustration."

The brainstorming session pointed to a previously unvoiced need of Mrs. C's. She was not having her sexual needs met by her husband. She never complained to her husband about her unfulfilled needs nor identified sex as a problem. The brainstorming information led to a new focus in problem solving.

A second example of creative thinking to solve personal problems involves a married couple who complained of mutual jealousy. Both were professionals who traveled some in their jobs. Both suffered from jealous feelings when the other left town. They identified their discomfort as a depression and worry when either spouse left. They decided that their goal was to develop mutual trust so that the spouse staying at home would be able to continue in his or her day-to-day task in comfort.

The responsibility issue was discussed. After each understood responsibility for feelings, Mrs. Connell stated the problem to be solved in this way: both of them wanted to *increase their own security in the relationship*.

Since both were bright and creative, I suggested creative thinking as a technique to solve their problem. After they had exhausted all their logical suggestions, I asked for a book title containing a paradox that would capture the essence of their goal of internal security. A period of silence was followed by a suggestion from Mrs. Connell, *Kinetic Stability*. I asked her to tell me more about the title.

"Security to me means stability. And a paradox would be movement of some kind. So kinetic—*Kinetic Stability*."

"Give me an example of kinetic stability from the world of manmade things."

"A fountain," suggested Mr. Connell. "A fountain is stable and constant but always moving."

"A flag, because it is a symbol of strength, flying high and fluttering in the wind," suggested Mrs. Connell.

"A gyroscope," continued Mr. Connell.

"Be a gyroscope and describe your experience," I instructed.

"Well—I feel real strong inside. There is a smooth whirling hum in me that always keeps me stable. If someone pushes me or tilts me, I always return to straight-up position. I can guide ships that are bigger and stronger than me but are not as stable as me. I can furnish the stability and direction for the whole ship, even in rough seas."

"Okay, now fit the concept of a gyroscope to your goal of being secure and not jealous."

This excursion away from the original complaint led to Mrs. Connell identifying a *trigger phrase* related to her insecurity—"My father did it." She developed a plan to deal with this phrase.

Thoughts That Control Feelings

Most feelings, at least in the adult, have a thought somewhere in the sequence of events leading up to the feeling. For example, Bob over the years has developed a conditioned response to figures of authority; however, he is not likely to produce that conditioned emotional response independent of thought. In the first place, in order for the authority figure to be perceived as an authority—a stimulus for emotional reaction—Bob has to put some mental label on him. Once the person is labeled as an authority and the chain of events is begun, Bob is likely to have fantasies of future difficulties with the authority figure and therefore escalate his feelings.

If we learn to manipulate the thinking part of the sequence, we will be capable of changing the feelings or maybe even preventing the feelings from occurring. This is a powerful skill.

In generating our feelings, either good or bad, or in conducting a problem-solving search for a desirable response, we all engage in inner speech. This inner speech may be partially out of our awareness; but in any case we continue to think, remember, predict, and tell ourselves to do something or not do something. All of these processes have an effect on our behavior and feelings.

In the very young child this speech is still externalized. It is not unusual to hear a young boy tell himself not to do something or give himself directions in order to get something done. As adults, we internalize the speech and may not be consciously aware that it is occurring as we go about our day-to-day tasks.

Much of psychotherapy is based on controlling and directing clients' inner speech. One particular therapy developed by Albert Ellis—rational emotive therapy—focuses almost entirely on what Ellis believes is an irrational inner speech that develops into neurosis. His focus is to teach rational kinds of thoughts (inner speech) that are incompatible with neurotic irrational motives.

Fantasy exercises are one of the most efficient ways of allowing us to increase our awareness of this experiential model of reality. When we are blocked in our thinking, we may get past the block by giving ourselves permission to make up an idea or to have a fantasy that does not have to be proven before it is expressed. Fantasy and imagination are very helpful in getting nonproductive individuals to produce ideas from their models of reality.

Fantasy Exercises

Find a comfortable place to sit down and relax. Allow yourself to have the following fantasy after you have read over the content.

Imagine that you are as free as you want to be—free to behave as you want to. Picture yourself in a number of day-to-day activities being as emotionally free as you wish to be. Make sure that you include fantasies of work situations, family situations, and social situations. Now after you have fantasized yourself being free as you want to be, decide what beliefs, rules, emotions, or skill deficits are preventing you from being this free. Give the block a physical form and develop a dialogue with what is blocking you. For example, if you told yourself you were not as free as you want to be because you are afraid, you might develop a picture of your fear sitting opposite you in a chair. I had one client who pictured her fear as a little reddy-kilowatt type of character sitting opposite her, and she saw him as being quite a nervous individual. In the dialogue with your block, find out the origin of the block and get as much information as you can to deal with the problem. Finally, figure out a creative way to problem solve related to the situation that is blocking you.

A second fantasy may aid in developing goals for changing something about yourself. Again find a comfortable place and relax. Close your eyes and imagine that you are walking up to a large building. A sign on the outside of the building announces that you are entering the Exchange Store. In the Exchange Store you can take any one characteristic of yourself that you don't like and exchange it for any other characteristic that you desire. As you walk through the store, you look around on the shelves and you see all sorts of interesting characteristics, such as assertiveness, friendliness, love, heartiness, creativity. You also see a chute going down to the basement—the place to discard your unwanted characteristic. Take your time and wander through the store. Make sure that you give up what you don't want and that you acquire what you do want.

Again, this fantasy allows you to get into your fantasy experience without the blocks of staying in touch with what you think you should want to give up and should acquire. Once you decide which characteristics you wish to eliminate or acquire, you can then make a plan to accomplish your goals.

"Make Up Something"

I will end with my most powerful confrontation to blocks in productive thinking—"Make up something." I use this phrase every day, several times. There may be some initial resistance by the client who thinks that "made up" material won't be relevant. However, thinking of an option and making one up both involve the same process. The latter carries with it an important difference—a permission. What is labeled "made up" does not have to be "good," "perfect," "relevant," or even "rational." What follows the permission is close to brainstorming and is more quickly set into action.

For example:

Client: "My boss expects more of me than I have time to do."

Therapist: "That sounds like a problem to be solved, Henry. What are you going to do?"

Client: "I just don't know. I'm afraid to tell him I can't handle it."

Therapist: "So are you stuck? Have you stopped thinking of alternatives?"

Client: "Yes. I have thought of everything and nothing seems to work. I mean, I haven't thought of anything I want to take a chance doing. He is such a hard worker himself."

Therapist: "You have run out of fresh ideas—so, *make something up.*"

Client: "What do you mean?"

Therapist: "I am more interested in your breaking the habit of not thinking right now than in the result of your thinking. So it's okay to make up something."

Client: "I see (pause). Well, I could be honest and tell him what I could realistically do. I could easily show him how much I do now. He probably hasn't thought of my workload."

Therapist: "Good. What about your fear? Will that be a stopper for you?"

Client: "I really think that the fear is unrealistic. He is a reasonable man. And you have already taught me that I don't have to wait on the feeling to go away before I do something about it."

I can add a personal note. Telling myself to make something up has gotten me through many thinking blocks. Even though I know beforehand that the thinking following the phrase is the same as that preceding, the permission gives me a new freedom I was not allowing myself.

Summary

Awareness covers the activities of gathering and processing information for problem solving through our senses and by thinking and feeling. Productive thinking involves generating alternatives when a problem is confronted and selecting the most probable of the alternatives. Nonproductive thoughts consist of worries and trigger phrases that cause unnecessary bad feelings.

Feelings may be useful in problem solving if they motivate action or reinforce problem-solving habits. However, feelings may also interfere with solutions if they are learned as a stereotyped reaction to stress and do not lead to action.

Chapter 6

Verbal and Nonverbal Behavior: What Are You Saying About Yourself?

Our behavior is that part of ourselves which is public. It is through what we do and what we say that other people know us. Much of our behavior is habitual. Current stimuli in our environment will likely activate a portion of our previous experience with that stimuli, and we will behave automatically and most often without awareness. Most of our day-to-day problems are solved with this kind of habitual behavior. The likelihood is that each element of our experience has a corresponding behavior that may be called forth by environmental stimuli. That is, every attitude, belief, thought, and feeling have an associated behavior that is meant either to solve a problem with which we have had previous experience or to communicate information to another person.

Passive Behaviors

We learn by modeling, trial and error, or instruction those behaviors that lead to need satisfaction or tension reduction, that is, solutions to problems. We also learn behaviors that *do not* contribute to problem solving. These behaviors are usually learned by escape from stress at the expense of long-term need satisfaction. *Passive behaviors are those behaviors that do not contribute to the solution of problems creating discomfort, although they may give temporary relief.* That is, these behaviors, in the long run, create more problems than they solve.

Martin Seligman has researched "learned helplessness" in animals: "Animals learn helplessness when they are exposed to uncontrollable and unpleasant events. . . . After such exposure they become so passive that they fail to take advantage of possibilities for escape when these present themselves." Seligman found that humans also become passive when exposed to inescapable noise. He noticed a similarity of their behavior to that of the depressed patient. "Both had difficulty in seeing that their responses were effective, both had low self-esteem, less aggression and less appetite. . . . Freud believed depression is anger turned inward; at least one subclass of human depression results from knowing that anger is useless in the face of uncontrollable trauma."

Passive behaviors, leading to an accumulation of problems, can be learned as a reaction to stress. My observation is that individuals in passive behaviors may be categorized into three levels. Each level relates to the number and/or emotional intensity of the unsolved problems. The levels were influenced by Jacqui Schiff's work.

Level I behaviors have as their focus to *feel better without solving the problem*. At this level we do nothing actively to solve our problems, and instead we may have *hope*. Hope helps us deal with "insurmountable" (insurmountable at our current functioning) problems. To give up hope or become hopeless is seen as disastrous. "Keeping your hopes up" is seen as healthy, positive functioning. If hope is accompanied by action, it may be helpful. However, hope by itself is a passive behavior. We hope that "time heals all wounds." We hope that "someone else will solve our problems." We hope that "things always get better if we wait long enough." We hope, we wait, we remain passive, and we *do nothing* about our problem.

A second alternative, as we do nothing, is to daydream. We have fantasies of success, being "discovered," winning the sweepstakes, making the "one big deal." Our fantasies are partially satisfying and tension relieving but passive.

A third passive "out" is to blame others for our responsibility and power in exchange for the relief of not having to act in our own behalf. Blame is different from taking responsibility to confront others with their mistakes to solve the problem. Blame is passive and seldom leads to problem solving. When we successfully blame others for our problems, we give away all of our motivation to solve those problems.

A different passive approach, but still at the first level, involves focusing on "what someone else wants for me." In this position we have given up on getting what we want out of life—we may not know what we want. For example, I once treated a physician in the third year of his residency (eighth year in medical education) who told me he never wanted to be a doctor. He "endured" his profession because that's what his mother had always dreamed of for him.

In focusing on another's goal for ourselves, we may wish to please the other person by doing what he or she wants or we may wish to rebel. In rebellion we keep someone else from attaining his or her goal (for us) and gain power over the other person's feelings. In either case, the focus is on the goals of someone else—not on our own goals.

Level II behaviors result from continued problem accumulation. The essence of Level II is that *feelings are strong and override thinking*. Instead of thinking, we do something to rid ourselves of the rising discomfort. The feeling itself is agitation, sometimes described as an "antsy" feeling.

We may *tap our feet or fingers, pace, wring our hands* to relieve tension. We may act on impulse, often using poor judgment. We may repeat a behavior that isn't working over and over (although the behavior may have worked at one time) because it is the "right thing to do" or because we don't "know what else to do." We may use *alcohol, drugs, overeat, smoke,* or *masturbate* to control the discomfort. Signs that we are at Level II include *worry* and *suffering,* both passive behaviors coupled with a magical belief that, if either is done enough, the problem may go away or someone else will recognize our discomfort and do something for us.

Level II behaviors communicate to others that something is wrong and that we need help. Passive people may in fact be rescued, delaying their solving the problems creating the discomfort. For example, a man may harbor accumulated problems related to self-esteem and his parents. He may recognize that "something is wrong" and take a vacation to "get away from his trouble." The result in fact is but temporary relief. (Aspirin marketing capitalizes on such relief.)

Level III behavior focuses on *forcing someone else to take responsibility and take care of us.* We may incapacitate ourselves or become violent. Our society will not tolerate either condition without taking over responsibility to *do something* to stop the crisis.

If we become violent in our job setting, our fellow workers will immediately take responsibility to control our actions. If they are unable to contain our violence, the local police will be summoned. If the police can't handle us, the National Guard will be called in, and so on, until we are in control. By our violence, we will have forced others to be responsible for our behavior, to take care of us. However, we may not like the kind of "care" we receive.

Incapacitation may take many forms: excessive use of alcohol or drugs, a nervous breakdown, physical exhaustion, suicidal gesture, hopelessness and extreme despair, severe headaches, refusing to get out of bed, psychosomatic or hysterical conversion reactions (some part of the body loses its function without physical basis).

All of us are subject to occasional passive positions in a problem situation, although Level III is rarely seen in most of the population. Good problem solvers can recognize their passive behaviors and can follow this recognition with a plan for solving their problems.

Driver Behaviors

Attitudes in the belief system have corresponding behaviors. A more accurate statement is that constellations of behaviors are "labeled" and a corresponding attitude is inferred. Some mental health professionals think, "Who needs the label and inference? Just deal with the behavior." This argument has merit. However, in teaching and training the layman, the labels help in organizing and discriminating those behaviors to be changed.

Taibi Kahler (refer to Chapter 4) has very carefully observed and recorded behaviors he associates with the inferred driver attitudes about our self-worth. The behaviors associated with the drivers have multiple functions. First of all, we use these behaviors to solve a particular problem relating to our self-worth. These behaviors *do work*—temporarily. If we desire to be "pleased" by others (agreed with), the Please Me behaviors will invite that response. That's why the behaviors persist. They are reinforced many times per day, and on a schedule of partial reinforcement. Behavioral researchers have found that behaviors reinforced on an occasional basis are more resistant to extinction when the reinforcement stops than those behaviors reinforced every time.

Second, these behaviors communicate to those observing our behavior what kind of behaviors we expect from them, if they are to remain "worthwhile" in our eyes. Culturally, we all are exposed to these nonverbal communications. That is, we know them already. However, we have not put Kahler's labels on them.

For example, while at a large party, I was with a group of friends. I felt relaxed and free to "be myself." A person approached our group. The group behavior changed. We stiffened, changed the tone of our voice, the content of our conversation. Although I had not met the newcomer, my behavior changed also. I noticed after a few minutes that his behaviors fit both the Be Perfect and the Be Strong drivers. He had behaviorally signaled his expectation that we put up a front and behave correctly. We could have avoided his invitation to change our behavior to meet his expectations, but we didn't.

Below the behaviors associated with the individual drivers are listed.

Be Perfect

When we are in the Be Perfect driver, everything we do must be perfect, no matter how long it takes or how difficult the task. Even our language must be of the highest quality. We use big words instead of smaller, simpler ones.

We also expect others to follow our high standards. No matter how well we do a task, we should have done it better. If we reach 99 percent perfection, we worry about the 1 percent of imperfection. We generally give more information than we are asked to give. We want to be understood perfectly with no chances of misinterpretation. We cannot tolerate the mistakes of others, and we feel compelled to correct them. If we say something negative about a person, we balance the picture by saying just as much positive and vice versa.

We always qualify what we say—using words like, "I think," "perhaps," or "maybe." If anyone disagrees with what we say, we have the "out" of saying, "I just thought it was so; I really didn't take a close look" or "I said maybe." This is a way we remain perfect.

When in a Be Perfect driver, our voice tone is likely to be well modulated and very demanding. Gestures might include counting on the fingers, steepling with the hands, scratching the head, lifting the index finger, and occasional pointing. The posture is very erect and rigid. Facial expression is often severe. People in this driver maintain a manner that is commanding, dominant, intellectual, and aggressive.

Hurry Up

When we are in a Hurry Up driver, we want what we want *right now*. We detest waiting on people. We feel a pressure to get things over with, and we never have enough time. We may speak so rapidly and with so much pressure that others fail to understand us. We may start at the last minute and arrive late or arrive early and wait on others. Either way, we may "get nervous" about it. We would rather do a job ourselves than wait on someone else's time schedule.

We may interrupt others who can never talk fast enough for us. We are usually thinking ahead to the next thing we have to do or say before we are finished with the last task.

When things don't go fast enough for us, we may pat our feet or tap our fingers nervously. Our voice tones may fluctuate up and down in a tremulous and impatient manner. Our gestures include many squirms, finger taps, pacing back and forth, and moving legs if we are sitting. Our posture includes frequent changes and quick movements. Our eyes may quickly dart back and forth. We may have an overall worried look on our faces.

Be Strong

In the Be Strong driver we often say, "I don't care" or "It really doesn't matter to me." We don't want anyone to know what we really think or feel. We always avoid displays of any emotion, especially crying. It is important that other people do not know how they affect us, so we never show if we are feeling put down. We accept most things in silence. We never ask for help or for things we really want. We have to do everything all by ourselves.

We have developed some bodily movements or postures or muscle tensions that shut off our feelings (this idea will be further developed in Chapter 9.) We may lean back in our chairs and push our toes against our shoes; we may tense certain muscle groups so that we drain off feelings that we don't want others to observe. Our voice tone will be strong and monotonous. We will demonstrate rigid hands and crossed arms. We may cross our legs and sit without much movement. Our facial expressions are likely to be strong, hard, cold— sometimes described as stone-faced.

Please Me

In a pleasing driver we believe that we are responsible for making those around us feel good; therefore, we look for what pleases them. It is important that we figure out what others want before they ask.

We may never say so, but we will also be disappointed if people we are pleasing don't take the same responsibility for pleasing us. We need approval from others and must continually check out how we are doing with them.

We will seldom deny a request, even if we don't want to do it. It is important to us to be known as the "good guys." We will use phrases like "would you," "could you," "you know," "you see," "do you understand," and "please."

When we want an agreeing response from someone else, we will load the dice by nodding yes with our eyebrows up and forehead wrinkled, signaling the answer we expect. Our voice tone may have peaks and valleys with a lot of whining. We are often described as being seductive and may take on the characteristics of begging.

Try Hard

In a Try Hard driver we will measure the value of things by the amount of effort required. We believe that life is a struggle requiring a great deal of effort on our part. We also enjoy making others try harder— perhaps by speaking too softly or too rapidly. Or when we talk, we may beat around the bush or go off on a tangent. We procrastinate frequently. We accept more responsibilities than we have time to fulfill. If someone else is hard to convince, we exert a great deal of effort to convince him.

Our favorite phrases are "I'll try," "I wish," "I want to," "I should," and "I can't." Our body posture may include leaning foward with elbows on knees. We will have firm gestures and often moving fists. Our brows will be slightly wrinkled, and we may have a puzzled look. Individuals in a Try Hard driver may talk a good deal about confusion and get into corners where there is no workable solution.

When Driver Behaviors Fail

What happens when the driver behaviors don't work for you? For example, you may be signaling behaviorally that you expect to be "pleased" and you will "please" in return. However, the person with you either does not please you or shows displeasure or both.

When the driver "fails," you begin to feel not worthwhile or not okay. In the driver training stage, you received some kind of disappointment, censure, or punishment. Kahler calls this phase a *stopper position*; that is, the driver has been stopped. The person administering the censure or punishment seems powerful and okay, so the stopper existential position is, "I'm not okay; you (the punisher) are okay." In the stopper position you may experience one or more of the following:

1. Picture yourself as inadequate
2. Be confused
3. Feel anxious
4. Feel depressed
5. Worry
6. Feel guilty
7. Be afraid

After the appropriate "bad feeling" at the stopper position, you may return immediately to a driver. A second choice is to proceed to another of the "bad feeling" stages.

Kahler hypothesizes a third phase (following the driver and stopper phases)—the *vengeful child*. This phase includes a switch to the other person being "not okay." The emotion is anger; the behavior is blame, put-down, sarcasm, one-upmanship. This phase is a defense against the more uncomfortable feelings of the

stopper phase. I remember using a behavior modification technique to overcome a specific fear by instruct-
ing the individual to "get angry" in the presence of the
fearful situation. Anger will cover up the feelings included in the stopper phase.

The fourth position is a "give up" position. In this
position the experience is one or more of the following:

1. What's the use?
2. The situation is hopeless.
3. I am helpless to do anything about it.
4. I am in a corner where I am "damned if I do and
   damned if I don't."
5. I am lonely and rejected.
6. I'm not okay and no one else is okay.

A vicious cycle is set up in which you decide to en-
sure self-worth by driver behavior, fail and go to one or
more of the bad feeling positions, experience a loss of
self-worth, and return to a driver or drivers to reestab-
lish self-worth.

This cycle can be stopped by stopping the driver behaviors and *allowing* an incompatible attitude. The incompatible "allowers" and behaviors are presented in
the last chapter.

Life-Styles and Drivers

The behavioral constellations labeled with the four
life-styles are presented in Chapter 4. In reviewing the
life-style behaviors and the driver behaviors, there are
many similarities. I have made some preliminary in-
vestigations of possible correlations between the two.
My observations were based on limited data (N=50),
and the instruments from which the data were gener-

ated were not standardized. Therefore, the following discussion signifies trends, not well-controlled studies.

Theorist life-style's highest correlation is negative. Theorist correlates negatively with the Hurry Up driver and positively with the Try Hard driver. There is a trend toward a negative correlation with Be Perfect and a positive correlation with Be Strong.

Thinker style also produces a high negative correlation with the Try Hard driver and a trend toward a negative correlation with Please Me. There is a positive correlation with both the Be Perfect and the Hurry Up drivers.

Feeler style is positively correlated with the Please Me and negatively correlated with the Be Perfect drivers.

Pragmatist style does not differentiate well from the thinker style. However, the pragmatist has high negative correlation with Please Me and no correlation with Try Hard. Both the Hurry Up and Be Perfect correlations are highly positive.

With further study we may determine that favorite drivers determine the development of particular life-styles.

Language as Model of Your Experience

The words we use comprise a major element in social process. We can tell others about our private experiences, what we want, and how we think and feel. With language, we also fool others, distorting our thoughts and feelings. Complex verbal communication is the major factor that separates us from lower animals. It is also a powerful tool in problem solving, as well as one of the most frequent problems that clients complain of.

"I can't communicate with my son/daughter/husband/ wife/boss . . . " is a statement often voiced.

Thinking would be difficult if we had no language with which to structure and label our experience. In fact, abstraction would be impossible without language. What we experience (in awareness) is codified in our native language. Our ability to perceive new experiences is determined by our language capacity.

A Headstart worker told me about his work with children who had a poverty of learning experience. He reported that the children at first showed no preference for different flavored (or colored) lollipops. They simply asked for candy. When they learned words to discriminate the different colors, they began to ask for a yellow one or a red one, distinguishing flavors that they associated with the colors.

The primary use of language, then, is to label and represent our experience; the secondary use, to communicate. Richard Bandler and John Grinder indicate: "This use of language, to communicate, is actually a special case of the use of language to represent. Communication is, in this way of thinking, the representation to others of our representation to ourselves. In other words, we use language to represent our experience—this is a private process. We then use language to represent our representation of our experience—a social process."

Miscommunication occurs when we fail to describe completely (through communication) our internal representation or when we delete significant information. This problem is compounded by the fact that the person to whom the communication is directed *fills in* the deleted portion from his or her own experience. Unless both persons' experience around the deletion is similar, a miscommunication takes place.

For example, John says to Bill, "I have had unbelievable mechanical problems with my car. It has been in the shop three times this month already." (John has deleted "and I want your sympathy.") Bill listens to John's representation and fills in the deleted part as "and I want your advice." Bill answers, "Never buy a foreign car, John. Nobody in town can repair them." John did not get the sympathy he wanted, and he didn't want to hear that he had made a mistake in choosing a foreign car. Bill thought he was giving John the advice sought, and he feels uneasy about the frustrated look on his friend's face.

Because our language is a verbalized representation of our experiential makeup, it is extremely helpful for us to analyze our internal representations when problem solving. In the case of psychotherapy, a client's language is a significant observable clue to his or her experiential makeup.

Cleaning Up Your Language

There are a number of words in the English language that are usually stimuli for internal reactions (feelings) or behaviors which are incompatible with solutions. For example, when you think silently or say, "I'll try," you actually ready yourself to expend energy without an expectation of results. In the statement, "I'll try my best," the deleted portion is usually "but don't necessarily expect much result from my efforts." The word "try" is a block to a commitment. (A commitment to change a behavior is further developed in Chapter 7.)

Consider the following list of words—how you use them, what you really mean, and how they interfere with problem solving.

Can't may have validity if you are considering flying without the use of an airplane. However, "can't" is often used to imply an inability to control your thoughts, feelings, or behaviors. "Can't" is often an important word in a trigger phrase—for example, "I can't stand it" or "You can't make me." (See Chapter 4.)

"Can't" used to imply an inability to control yourself is a cop-out, a way to avoid change, and therefore invalid. You likely mean "won't," which is a decision on your part. "Won't" is a much more powerful word to use here because it leaves you with the option of making a new decision—"I will."

Can will improve your problem-solving position by replacing the word "can't." Every child who has read the story of the puffing little engine who continually repeated "I think I can, I think I can" knows the value of "can." However, "can" does not mean that you *will* do anything—only that you can and that you may still decide not to.

I attended the New Orleans jazz festival in the spring of 1977. Many different performers were playing on separate stages scattered around the grounds. One could stroll past the various musicians, pausing or sitting on the ground when the performer was particularly interesting. Bongo Joe was alone on a stage, whistling, singing, and tapping his fingers on tremendous drums. Some of his lyrics follow: "*Can?* Can don't mean shit, man. *Will.* Will is where it's at. Will means, got to."

Bongo Joe's philosophy has value in the making of a commitment to problem solve. When an individual's behavior is important to me, I am less interested in what he can do; I want to know what he will do. Saying "I want to," "I wish," or "I would like to" are all means of avoiding a *will* decision.

Should occurs with high frequency in your day-to-day life. When you give or ask for advice and when you instruct others, you depend heavily on "shoulds." However, "should" suggests an unreal condition. The focus is shifted from what *is* to what *should* be. Properly, the word "should" sets a standard to work toward; however, when past behavior is being discussed, unhealthy guilt feelings usually follow—unhealthy because the past cannot be changed. Saying "I should have done better" can be a statement of observance and invite a decision to do something differently in the future. On the other hand, it can be a statement inviting remorse and guilt.

If your "should" helps you in future problem solving, keep it; if it is of no value, drop it.

Hope is something you are not supposed to lose or give up. To be hopeful is to maintain an optimism for the future and a motivation to keep going. However, using the word "hope" is too often a passive maneuver, a shifting of responsibility to an outside source and waiting for something to happen. "I hope things get better" or "I hope people stop pushing me around" or "I hope I am not boring you" are all statements that imply waiting, taking no action. Hoping, in this context, is a nonproductive alternative to thinking of viable solutions.

But, as a conjunction, is used to connect two separate

and complete sentences that express facts of opposite tendency. Thus the effect of "but" is to oppose the first idea presented.

In the sentence, "I like your idea, but I would add this," the "but" negates the liking of the idea. The intended communication could be more appropriately expressed, "I like your idea, and I would add this." Joining the ideas with "and" does not detract from liking the idea.

Always and *Never* are designed to create emotion by expressing an extreme. Parents use these words to control their children, and later children turn them back on their parents. "You have forgotten to do what I told you to do two times this month" does not carry the impact of, "You always forget what I tell you." "You never bring me a present, Daddy," is more powerful than, "It has been a week since you brought me anything."

"Always" and "never" are favorite rule-making words of parents. "You *always* be polite and *never* talk back," a parent instructs. If the child now grown into the adult follows this advice, he or she may be passive and not stand up for his or her rights.

All of this may sound like an inapplicable lesson in semantics. However, cleaning up your language leads to problem solutions and straight talk when communicating with others. Talking straight involves using clear, concise, uncluttered communication. Donald Gibson provides an example of how not to communicate in a humorous exaggeration of a treatment contract: "I thought I might like to try to make a little progress in exploring why ya can't seem to be able to learn how to be more free of your problems."

Healthy Behavior

Psychologists have been criticized for having more data on abnormal than on normal behavior. A client of mine once set a goal to change his homosexual urges to heterosexual urges. He was "turned on" by men although he had never engaged in a homosexual act. He was successful in getting aroused by women. One day he asked me, "What is the normal urge or sexual thought per day. What standard am I shooting for?" I had no idea.

What is healthy problem-solving behavior? I will answer that question in two ways: (1) those problem-solving behaviors that differentiate a normal from a clinical population and (2) those behaviors and skills I have set as standard criteria for the completion of solution training.

A few years ago I developed a questionnaire to assess problem-solving skills. I included a number of questions I considered relevant to good problem solving. I gave the questionnaire to two different populations: clients from my industrial consultation and clients who came in for treatment of neurotic and a few psychotic disorders. Only one question differentiated the two populations: "List as many options or actions toward solving the problem as you can think of, in the order of most preferred to least."

The most disturbed of my clients would list none, one, or two options, while the more functional of my clients would average around four (I indicated space on the answer sheet for ten options). These observations are related to the recycle phase on the problem-solving flowchart (Figure 1). Healthy behavior involves doing something else toward solving problems if the last action didn't work. Sometimes continued new actions depend on a new problem definition to generate new alternatives. Unhealthy behavior involves repeating a behavior that has not worked, giving up altogether, or some other passive behavior.

The second approach to a definition of healthy behavior involves developing criteria for acceptable problem-solving skills: "When do you graduate from solution training?" These criteria are still in a developmental stage since I have yet to answer all my own questions regarding a useful standard.

The first discovery I made was that having only one standard for all my clients was not realistic. People come to learn problem-solving skills from different backgrounds and skill levels. Also clients have different goals, some short-term and specific-problem oriented and some long-term and personal-growth oriented. I developed different levels of criteria to satisfy different needs. These goals are discussed with my clients at about the third session. Earlier goal setting is difficult because the clients lack knowledge about the goals.

Criteria for Completion of Solution Training

Basic Level

1. The original complaint has been satisfied by a measurable change (or problem has been redefined).
2. The client is knowledgeable about responsibility for feelings and demonstrates this knowledge by his or her verbal behavior in the training session.

3. The client can identify when he or she is in a passive behavior and can switch to taking action.
4. The client can demonstrate accurate problem defining (two-chair technique) and can switch to a second definition.

Intermediate Level
1. The client has demonstrated competence at the Basic Level.
2. The client can identify driver behavior and can stop his or her top two drivers in the training session.
3. The client has identified rules in his or her belief system related to the complaint, identified the associated trigger phrases, and developed a new behavioral-thinking-feeling sequence following each phrase.
4. The client demonstrates the ability, unassisted, to overcome blocks in thinking.
5. The client has knowledge of time management and self-management.
6. The client can demonstrate assertive skills in handling aggressive people and passive people.
7. The client can demonstrate the problem-solving sequence, by the two-chair method, with any problem presented.
8. The client has significantly reduced redefining reality in sessions.
9. The client has controlled or has a strategy to deal with emotions that interfere with problem solving.

Advanced Level
1. The client has demonstrated competence at the Intermediate Level.

2. The client has stopped all drivers in the training session (okay if prompt is needed).
3. The client has demonstrated ability to identify significant belief system rules and their associated trigger phrases in a wide range of life situations.
4. The client has demonstrated the ability to role play all the life-styles—appropriate to different circumstances.
5. The client has developed clear life goals toward personal growth and is actively pursuing these goals.

My first thought was that the minimum criterion would be to make the necessary changes to satisfy the original complaint. This change is certainly important. However, I found that many times my clients redefine their problem, maybe several times, so that the original complaint is no longer the major issue. For example, one client's original goal was "to change so my father (and also her boss) will be proud of me instead of criticizing all the time." By the end of treatment, her father was somewhat less critical but never expressed pride or complimented her performance. However, she set and achieved goals in learning time management, in developing assertive skills, and in redefining her self-worth on a basis other than her father's approval.

Almost all clients complete the Basic Level when they remain in treatment with that goal. Most clients set Intermediate Level as a goal. A few clients have moved into Advanced Level, but no one has completely satisfied the criteria. Advanced Level has some high standards. For example, I have not stopped all my driver behaviors in session. And as conditions change, new elements of our belief systems cause problems. These change needs in the belief system are open-ended. Criterion four in The Intermediate Level is useful and attainable and may belong at Level II.

With all their faults, these criteria are a beginning, and revision is possible. The greatest fault of the psychotherapist is to have no criteria in mind or to be unable to communicate the criteria to a client.

Chapter 7

Changing Your Behavior: Self-management

Man is "so smart today that he controls almost all of nature except his own nature," writes Walter Judd. Self-control is a goal that many of us strive for—and yet never reach. New Year's resolutions are more frequently broken than kept. "I don't have any willpower" is an often-voiced complaint when we eat, smoke, or drink more than we "should" and put off doing what we "ought" to do.

Willpower is generally thought of as an internal strength that allows us to pass up a smaller but immediate desire for gratification of our needs to reach a larger, more satisfying long-term goal. What most of us experience in our desire to change might better be termed "wish power." We hope for a change and do little else. We *wish* that our immediate desire, which will create future problems (overweight, a hangover, a missed deadline), would magically disappear.

Ineffective willpower (wish power) is knowing you shouldn't do something that you want to do (or should do something that you don't want to do) and deciding to force yourself to go against your desires without a clear plan to deal with the basic "want to." A "should do" is poor control for a "want to" over a long period of time. Effective self-management, therefore, requires planning as follows:

1. Specify and label the behavior, thought, or feeling that you want to change.
2. Look for "stoppers" in making the change.
3. Make a clear commitment to change.
4. Write a contract.
5. Self-monitor.
6. Control the consequences of your old or new behavior.
7. Repeat and reward the new behavior until the new habit is established.

Stoppers to Self-Management

There are many internal and external events that may interfere with self-control. Your goal of managing a particular behavior will be more easily reached if you are aware of potential pitfalls. You can then prepare a plan to ward off possible blocks to goal attainment.

In a program of weight control, you may consider hunger as the chief deterrent to learning new eating habits. Working with weight control clinically, I have found a number of more important stoppers.

1. *Social pressure.* Dieters who are not assertive enough to let their friends and relatives know their determination to lose weight are subject to a barrage of social pressures: "Oh, no, I cooked your favorite— chocolate mousse—just for you" or "You're certainly not going to diet on Thanksgiving, are you?"

Seemingly well-meaning friends defeat diet regimes—most frequently when the dieter has a weak commitment to change.

2. *Anger.* Anger at oneself or at others often leads to excessive eating. Eating can be experienced as self-destruction or as aggression toward others. I remember a client who once locked herself in the bathroom and ate an entire case of cupcakes while her husband stood outside the door, pleading for her not to do it. Her act was one of aggression toward her husband. Depression or anxiety, as well as anger, are feelings that may also lead to eating binges.

3. *Boredom.* Boredom can be a strong drive to "do something." Eating is a way to structure one's time in a pleasurable activity.

4. *Fatigue.* Physical conditions such as fatigue can lessen any self-control activities.

5. *Alcohol.* Intoxication lowers control and allows one either to forget commitments or to disregard the importance of commitments. Drinking is also often associated with social situations involving other stoppers to weight control, such as convenience foods or social pressures.

6. *Dieting for someone else.* Losing weight for your husband, wife, or anyone else is doomed to failure. Any irritation with the other person, and no more diet! Or if you lose the weight and don't receive enough reward, well, gain it back!

7. *Convenience food.* Food that does not have to be prepared, those close-at-hand munchies, are often consumed before you are aware that the bag was opened.

8. *Erroneous future fantasies.* An idea that life will lack pleasure if you stick to the new eating habits is a stopper to change. Couple this idea with the belief that you will regain lost weight if you ever go off your diet, and you're really stuck.

Once you have identified the stoppers, a plan can be made to decrease the probability of their interference. Specific stoppers may be dealt with by learning specific techniques, such as assertiveness or time management. The remainder of this chapter, however, will develop several general techniques that lay a foundation for successful problem solving: labeling, making a commitment to change, writing a contract, self-monitoring, and setting up consequences. At times, I will directly address the therapist; however, this is not exclusive information. In life, we are our own most available and powerful therapists, so read on and get whatever information is useful.

Labeling

Internal experiences and associated behaviors may be vague and never verbalized to others or to ourselves. Putting labels on things allows us to structure our experiences, to identify in a context what our problem is or what the source of our problem is. For example, you may have a vague feeling of depression. You're not sure why you feel that way; not knowing what to do about it, you simply wait and hope that you'll feel better soon. Labeling the source of your feeling as Critical-Parent-produced or Victim-Role-produced (these terms are described below) allows you to identify what needs be changed.

Outlined below are two different applications of the

labeling process: the drama triangle and the six-chairs exercise. Transactional analysis theory is full of creative labeling potential; however, labeling of the same behavior may be done successfully from any theoretical orientation.

Drama Triangle

The four false beliefs outlined in Chapter 3—(1) Other people can make me feel bad, (2) Other people can make me feel good, (3) I can make other people feel bad, (4) I can make other people feel good—translate into three roles from which power plays are made—Persecutor, Rescuer, and Victim. Your favorite false belief is likely to indicate the power role in which you find yourself most frequently. If you believe that other people can make you feel bad by what they say or do, you are a victim looking for a persecutor. If you believe that others can make you feel good, you are a victim looking for a rescuer. If you believe that you can make other people feel bad, you are likely to get into the persecutor role and find a victim. If you believe that you can make other people feel good, you are likely to spend a good deal of time in the rescuer role. From your favorite role (or position on the drama triangle), you will initiate power plays; however, all persons eventually spend time in each of the three roles.

The drama triangle, sometimes called the Karpman Triangle for its creator Steve Karpman, is shown in Figure 3. Any dramatic event can be analyzed by identifying and labeling these three roles and looking for switches from one role to another. Dr. Karpman points out that these switches constitute the most exciting part of drama, the dramatic moment. Switches are emotionally arousing. The drama itself may take place in a television show, a book, a stage play, or your own living room.

Consider a television show in which a young girl (I'll call her Marie) falls in love. She takes on a "rescuer" role, wanting to feed and nurture her "victim" John. John, who is not particularly interested in Marie, accepts her dinner invitations and affection for awhile. It is a dramatic moment when John turns "persecutor" and decides to take advantage of Marie's generosity. At this point, Marie has switched from "rescuer" to "victim"—without doing anything.

Next Marie talks with her best friend, gets a different perspective on the situation, and becomes angry. In a scene with John, she turns "persecutor" and declares loudly and haughtily that he has made a fool of her. John spends a few moments in the "victim" role looking guilty and sad. Then as Marie breaks into tears, John puts his arm around her and begins to offer gentle, rescuing words.

End of show. To be continued tomorrow. Now, labeling John's and Marie's behaviors won't change anything for them. They can't change the up-and-down unpleasantness of their lives because they have a writer who makes his living creating the dramatic role switches for them to live. On the other hand, we write our own scripts, choose our own roles. Therefore, for contrast, consider the following scene in your own living room.

Here is a typical example of a living room drama triangle episode. Bob brings home a poor report card from his high school. His father has not been pleased with recent grades, and these are no better. In the past his father had given advice on studying and test taking,

DRAMA TRIANGLE

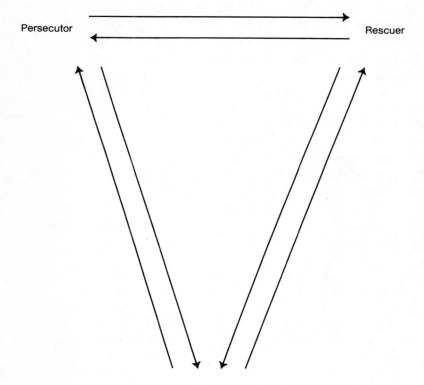

FIGURE 3

but Bob had insisted that his advice didn't work. Their arguments escalated, and both had felt angry and later guilty. Testings show that Bob has no learning disabilities. Today, Bob's father feels compelled to criticize and to go a step further—that is, he wants his son not only to improve his grades but also to "feel bad" about his poor report card. So he looks angry, shouts, and threatens punishment. They argue, and Bob runs away from home.

Both father and son are attempting to gain power and control over one another. The ultimate control is to control another's feelings. Most other controls (money, obedience) eventually refer back to a feeling state. Even giving over control of your feelings to someone else can be stimulating—a relief. Any emotional arousal, positive or negative, is potentially reinforcing; and this reinforcement increases the probability that the behavior which causes the arousal will be repeated. The potentially reinforcing effect of negative feeling states is demonstrated by lines of people waiting to watch *Jaws*, the pride with which people discuss a personal "confrontation," and the degree of internal excitement of a person shouting, "You S.O.B., I'm going to beat hell out of you." As mentioned in Chapter 1, we all need to be recognized, and this need may be fulfilled by positive or negative regard.

The father in the above case wants to relate differently to his son, but he feels unable to control his behavior. He doesn't know where to begin managing his own behavior. Once the father and his son have labeled their pattern of interaction, the two are in a position to set up a self-management program. As stated before, labeling of the same behavior may be done successfully from any theoretical orientation. The "true" label is not so important. To label and then to commit ourselves to deal with what is labeled is the key.

The drama triangle analysis goes like this: Father starts in the rescuer role, offering advice on studying and test taking. Bob starts in the victim role of making bad grades no matter how hard he tries. Father moves to the persecutor role and decides to punish and make Bob feel bad. Bob switches to the percecutor role and victimizes his father for not being understanding. Father feels guilty but covers his guilt with anger and moves back to the persecutor role. . . .

Being in a position to set up a self-management program doesn't mean that anything will necessarily happen. Many of us feel satisfied with labeling alone and go no further—and therefore, we do not change. After labeling, we as self-managers must make a plan to change what we are doing and proceed with stopping our unwanted behaviors.

In the case of Bob and his father, they set up consequences for their behavior. Both father and son agreed to pay the other one dollar when either pointed out a persecutor position of the other. Not only did this consequence make each individual more aware of his own behavior, it also served to break up the power play; if the "victim" gets a dollar, he doesn't feel in the victim role.

Other consequences—both positive and negative— were set up to aid Bob with study habits. For example: no study, no television. The consequences *were not* punishment because both parties were aware of them beforehand and because the consequences were administered without an accompanying attempt to make either feel bad.

In conclusion, the skill of labeling behaviors can be enhanced by rehearsing the persecutor, victim, and rescuer roles. When you can easily role play the persecutor, victim, and rescuer, you can more easily avoid all three.

Six Chairs

A second labeling and discrimination exercise based on transactional analysis involves splitting the traditional Parent, Child, and Adult ego states hypothesized by Eric Berne into six functional ego states as follows:

Arrange six chairs in a semicircle with one chair at the center, two chairs on the left, and three chairs on the right. The chairs represent six functional ego states (see Figure 4).

The exercise involves active discrimination and labeling of internal events and external behaviors. The individuals sit in the chair corresponding to his or her behavior, changing chairs as behavior changes. This exercise usually requires supervision until skills are developed in discriminating the feelings and behaviors corresponding to the ego states.

First, I will briefly describe the six functional ego states. When individuals seat themselves in the Adult chair, they are to think rationally without regard to what "should" be or to what they feel. They compute information in terms of probability of events. Facts are gathered and plans are generated to solve problems.

The three chairs on the right correspond to the Child ego state, functionally divided into the Natural Child,

SIX EGO STATES

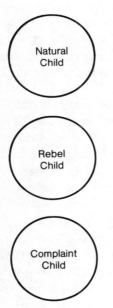

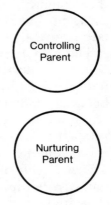

Figure 4

the Rebel Child, and the Compliant Child. The Natural Child feels excitement, experiences creativity and intimacy, and seeks comfort. On the negative side, the Natural Child is impulsive, self-centered, and impatient.

When the impatient Natural Child doesn't get immediate need satisfaction, the two other functional child states serve as adaptations to the (originally external) grown-ups who are setting limits. The Rebel Child, his own needs frustrated, can at least feel powerful by not doing what the adults want him to do. He gets angry and takes a "you can't make me" attitude. Or, more subtly, he responds, "I can't do it (ha, ha)." On the positive side, the Rebel Child has strength and refuses to be pushed around.

The second adaptation is labeled the Compliant Child. The characteristics grouped under this label include pleasing others—finding out what others want and doing it for them. When the Compliant Child thinks that he is not pleasing others, he may exhibit confusion or feel sad, afraid, or helpless.

The two chairs on the left represent the Parent ego state, functionally divided into the Controlling Parent and the Nurturing Parent. The Controlling Parent is limit-setting and, at times, punishing. This is the internal source of messages such as, "Don't do that, it will get you into trouble" or "You're stupid for wanting to do that." When this part of a personality is helpful, protection is furnished. When the Controlling Parent is hurtful, persecution occurs. The Nurturing Parent role is warm, loving, and permissive. In this role, rescuing and dependency invitations are common.

Becoming aware of the distinctions between the ego states is fundamental to the six-chair exercise. Knowing a label for the source of conflicting attitudes increases the probability of control or managing that aspect of your behavior, thinking, or feeling.

An example of the application of the six-chair exercise follows. A woman has been experiencing frequent anger at her boss. Her job is becoming endangered. Her original response to this is, "That's just my nature. I can't help it." In the six-chair exercise, she learns to label her feelings, thoughts, and behaviors (speaking from the appropriate chairs):

1. I am angry and responding from my Rebel Child.
2. I have the information that rebellion against someone else doesn't usually get me what I want (Adult).
3. I also know that I have five other roles I can use in relating to my boss, so I'm not stuck with the rebel response (Adult).
4. What is a way of responding (which I have discriminated and labeled) that has a better probability of meeting my needs?

The individual, having identified the ego state from which she wishes to respond to her boss, can plan to change. (This exercise ends with adult problem solving.)

Frequently, you will be unable to get into the role represented by one of the chairs. You may, for example, be deficient in nurturing skills. In everyday experiences, you know that under stress it is hard for you to give yourself verbal assurance and encouragement. In the six-chair exercise, either you do not know how to act when sitting in the Nurturing Parent chair, or you feel so uncomfortable in the nurturing role that your attempts are unsuccessful. In this case, you have identified and labeled a skill deficit in which you may be coached and trained.

In summary, labeling enriches experience to allow finer discriminations of behaviors, thoughts, and feelings. Labeling, then, puts you in greater control of yourself, ready to make a definite commitment to change. However, labeling can hinder problem solving, as well as help you to find a solution. Once a person or concept is labeled, you may respond to them as if they "were the label" and thus make mistakes as people or situations change. Prejudice stems from such labeling. A safe way to label as an aid in self-management is to label your own thoughts, feelings, and behaviors for monitoring and control. *Do not label others.* If what you are doing in a social situation is not working, discard old labels and reassess the behavior of the others involved. If you have labeled another person as a "persecutor" and are responding to him as such, you have based such a label on only a portion of his behavior and will be misperceiving the remainder of his behavior.

Commitment to Change

What kind of commitment is necessary for change? The key to changing is to make a valid decision to do something different. People more often make "halfway decisions" by leaving loopholes in what they decide. For example, a client wishing to control his smoking or drinking may fool himself with cop-out phrases, such as, "I'll try," "I want to," "I wish," or "I should." These phrases suggest the client will put out effort but expects a probable failure.

A client instructed to reduce his smoking to five cigarettes per day responds, "I really should do that. I'll try my best next week." If I, as his therapist, am unaware of how he is copping out, I might allow him to leave with a "loophole" commitment. The probability is that he will not meet and maintain his smoking goal, although he may keep his commitment. He may return the following week and bemoan that, even though he *tried* his best, he averages smoking one pack per day. If one listened closely, his commitment was only to *try to cut down*, not to in fact cut down at all. If my client or I still do not catch the loophole, he may commit himself to "try even harder next week."

He returns one week later smoking two packs per day. He has tried twice as hard "this time," which means he hassled more about it. He got "more nervous" and guilty, so he smoked more to quiet his nerves. If, however, I inform him of the fallacy of a "try" commitment and ask for a straight commitment in terms of what he "will do," he may refuse to give one. Just moments before, he made a commitment to "try his best" to cut down to five cigarettes. When penned down, he may state, "No, I won't say that I will do it. That's just too much to ask in one week's time." So he is quite easily convinced to try, even though he knows he won't, but he will not *make a clear commitment "to do it."*

Slicing the pie thinner, that is, suggesting ten cigarettes or fifteen, I eventually find a level at which he will make a definite commitment. Allowing a "try" sets him up to fail and to feel comfortable with failure because of the loophole. Finding his "will" level increases the probability of success, and in time he can reach the same five-cigarette level.

The "will" commitment creates a larger population of individuals who will be successful with their commitment. However, some of those making a "will" commitment still do not perform. A second loophole may be hidden even when the commitment seems to be a clear decision to perform. The decision may really be an "if" decision: "I will do it if . . . " A way to check out the "if" decision is to ask the client (or yourself) what he said to himself immediately after he made the statement, "Yes, I will do it." A number of these individuals will laugh and say, "Well, I just told myself that if my boss stays off my back (or some other similar environmental problem to them), then I will do it." Here again, a verbalized and firm commitment to me still left a loophole open. If I don't check out the loophole and he again has not met his commitment, he may upon returning let me in on the commitment that he made silently to himself. He will typically say, "Gee, I would have done it, but my boss was really a terror this week."

Written Contract

The strength of your commitment will be increased by a written contract. The leverage will be even stronger to the extent that you make your contract public information to your family and friends. Contracts should clearly specify the behavior or feeling to be changed and should include consequences for changing or not changing (when consequence is the form of motivation used).

You might ask, "Isn't it better to do it on your own without needing someone else to check on you?" I don't have any arguments with that particular statement. However, doing it on your own and failing is not in fact taking responsibility for yourself. If it is helpful to make your contract public, then do it and be successful. Later on you can work on the skill of doing it on your own and being successful. In making your contract public, you are not really looking for a rescuer. You are taking the responsibility for doing whatever is necessary for you to get on with life. If you do it correctly, you are not turning over this responsibility to someone else when you say to them, "Look, I'm going to lose two pounds this week, and it will be helpful in motivating me for you to know this and for me to be able to come to you next week and tell you that I have, in fact, lost two pounds."

Consequences

One of my colleagues was treating a young girl for enuresis. She wet the bed every night. He called on a number of different treatment techniques for her problem. In spite of all of his skills, she did not stop wetting the bed. So my colleague suggested that the child's mother take her to a urologist. The little girl did go to the urologist and he started the examination. He said to her, "Well, okay, now we are going to do an X-ray," and she asked, "What is that?" He said, "You get up on this table and we are going to take a picture of the inside of your body." She drew back, "I don't want to do that." "Well, you have to," he insisted. After a moment, she said, "I'll tell you what. I'll stop wetting the bed instead." And she did.

So, one way of bringing about change in yourself is to find out what your "X-ray machine" is; that is, what motivates you enough to make some meaningful redecisions about your life. If you are willing to do that, you can change your behavior.

In psychology the equivalent of the X-ray machine is called consequences. If you have a feeling or behavior that you wish to accelerate or decelerate, a good starting place is to look at the consequences of that behavior; that is, what happens next after the event to be changed occurs. For example, if every time you pout you get attention from your spouse when you may have been otherwise ignored, your spouse's attention is likely maintaining your behavior. If pouting is a real problem to you, if it leads to an angry, bitter day, then you could ask your wife to ignore it. Better still, on days you don't pout, your spouse can show you a great deal of interest.

Much of the time, the consequences maintaining behavior are unnoticed. In this case, a known consequence can be added to change the behavior in a desirable direction. The more immediate the reinforcer, the more effective the consequence. Some consequences are easier to apply immediately than others. For example, popping a rubber band that has been placed around your wrist will have an effect on thoughts that precede the mildly painful consequence. An individual with self-deprecating thoughts may decrease the frequency by the rubber band method.

When a consequence is not immediately under your control, a more distant (in time) reinforcer may be effective because the "thought" of the later consequence is in close time proximity with the behavior. However, because the more distant reinforcement may lessen the probability of self-management, the more immediate reinforcement is recommended. Working for the privilege of going on a vacation is less effective than working for a smaller weekly goal. Payoffs on a daily basis are more powerful than a weekly dinner and movie. One way to insure immediacy of reinforcement by later events is to have a fantasy of the event immediately following the behavior being reinforced.

Daily habits like brushing your teeth or using hot water to bathe are effective reinforcements. If you set up the negative consequence of giving up the privilege of brushing your teeth, you can still use mouth wash. Even with mouth wash, however, the grunge begins to grow in the afternoon. The unpleasantness increases the probability that you will earn the privilege of brushing your teeth the following day.

As an example, Barbara was very efficient in her job. She was both thorough and rapid in her work skills. However, her social skills were lacking. She was viewed by her coworkers as either a sourpuss or stuck-up. In fact, she was very shy and frightened in social relationships. She actively avoided attempts made by others to be pleasant. In time her fellow workers left her alone. She withdrew into loneliness although surrounded by people.

Barbara agreed to the following contract: "I agree to give at least one compliment (a compliment I feel that is deserved) per day for the first week to one of my fellow workers. I will increase the number of compliments, one per week, until I reach the level of ten compliments per day. By maintaining my quota each day, I will earn the privilege of brushing my teeth the following day. If I fail to meet my quota two days in a row, I will, in addition to not brushing my teeth, give up hot water for bathing." During the change program, Barbara increased her compliments to ten per day. Two weeks after the consequences were discontinued, the level of compliments averaged out around five per day. Barbara's program was successful. Although all of her social problems were not completely solved, Barbara had a successful social experience in a situation important in her daily life. She had made a significant change in her behavior on which she would build other changes.

I discovered a powerful reinforcer for middle-class women in 1970. A patient of mine came to her appointment more distraught than with her original crisis. As it turned out her maid was ill and wouldn't be coming to work. Her plans had been completely disrupted. I have used the "maid" consequence many times. For example, if a woman did not meet her weight-loss commitment, she called her maid and asked her not to come. In hard-core cases the husband would call the maid. The maid, however, received full pay. Maids love this consequence.

The most powerful consequence I have found for men is to have the wife let the air out of all four tires if they welch on their commitment. One problem with such powerful consequences is that some people drop the whole program after pumping up four tires with a bicycle pump. A general negative consequence that has been used by behavior modifiers for a number of years involves the writing of a series of checks to an organization the person "hates"—such as the Communist party or the Ku Klux Klan. If the client fails to meet the criteria, a check is sent to that organization.

However, the commitment to change is more meaningful than the above consequences. Without the commitment we will look for a way to avoid the consequences even if we must terminate treatment.

Self-monitoring

Knowledge of results is important in any change procedure, yet many of the people I aid in changing their behavior resist measuring their progress or lack of it.

The recording data is a bother and therefore avoided. People say they *know when they make the changes they want, so why measure?* Speculating about behavior change can lead us to erroneous conclusions. To avoid the pitfall, in the process of changing our behavior we must be good observers. One of the most accurate ways to observe what is happening is to record the number of times something happens in a given time period.

John has decided to control his anger. He has identified his anger as not leading to any useful action. He realizes that some of his anger is inappropriate and a problem to himself. He arranges a sound program to change his behavior but decides not to measure his anger correctly. He tells himself that he will "know" when he is less angry and therefore need not measure directly. Three weeks later John is angry—he is very angry. He also remembers being angry that morning as well as the day before. John is naturally discouraged. He decides to drop the whole program and learn to live with his "angry personality."

Should John have decided to observe and record his angry behavior directly, he would have observed that prior to the beginning of his program he experienced angry feelings an average of 12 times per day or .66 times per waking hour. Later, when he felt angry, he would not have been discouraged because he has reduced his anger to 2 felt angers per day. That is significant progress. These data will likely encourage John not only to maintain the program but also to feel good about his progress. In addition, now that his angers are down to a reasonable number, he is in a position to enter into assertive training to learn how to get his needs met without being overly aggressive or angry.

In the last example, how did John know his rate of "angries" at the start of the program? It is a good idea to get a baseline from which you can make judgments about your progress. The baseline is easily obtained by observing the behavior approximately one week before you begin your program (or for such a period of time that the behavior is relatively stable). If you are excited about the possibility of changing your behavior, waiting is hard. However, if you decide to wait (after all you are working on self-control), you will have more data on which to make your judgments. It is okay to reward yourself for waiting a week and "doing it right."

Ogden Lindsley, in the 1972 workshop on behavioral management in Kansas City, Kansas, found knowledge of results alone to be a potent reinforcer for both children and adults. He found that in some cases the consequence was a hindrance to change, whereas watching "progress" on a graph was a real "turn on." Lindsley's observation is another reason to record baseline data. If during the first week of observation the behavior continues to change in the desired direction, continue to monitor the behavior only. A consequence may not be necessary. In working with adults, self-monitoring of behavior and a clear commitment to change are powerful change techniques.

William was a salesman. He liked the independence of his job. He worked mainly out of the office with prospective customers. He was responsible for setting his own schedule. However, the independence was a two-edged sword, since William was a procrastinator. Whatever he decided to do, there were several less important tasks that he would do first. He was always busy but accomplished little meaningful work. William made a contract to monitor and record his procrastinations. If he thought about any one task and ended up doing another task first, that counted as one procrastination. With this definition of procrastination, he was averaging about 22 per day or about 3.6 per workday hour. He might chalk up 7 or 8 on one particular task. He would keep thinking about it but do something else first. William contracted to decrease his procrastination each day, with no consequences except his knowledge of progress. In three weeks he was down to an efficient range of 0 to 4 per day. His productivity increased manyfold.

Self-management is necessary to get yourself going on problems to be solved. Accepting the responsibility for feelings and behavior is only a half-job if you lack the skill to manage or control your feelings and behavior.

Chapter 8

It Takes Time to Solve Problems

A way in which all of us are equal regardless of station in life, financial status, or intelligence is that we all have twenty-four hours each day in which to structure our activities. "Time and tide wait for no man," the proverb goes. However, the decision as to how those twenty-four hours may be spent determines, to some extent, our success in life. An important part of self-management and the ability to solve problems is the capacity to decide and control how we will spend our time. Successful problem solvers are good managers of their time. I don't mean that every waking hour should be productive or accountable. Industries that stress production and ignore human resources soon have dissatisfaction and unhappiness among employees. There are useful ways to structure time other than being productive. Overachievers may miss much of what life has to offer if they focus on production only. However, those of us leaving the responsibility of how our time is spent to chance or decisions made by others may find our lives neither productive nor pleasurable.

Eric Berne wrote of *structure-hunger*, the problem of what to do with our time. People who have the skill to aid us in avoiding boredom by helping with time structure (such as entertainers) are highly paid in our culture. Boredom is a feeling state that motivates time structure. Berne divided time structure into six categories of activity: withdrawal, rituals, pastimes, games, intimacy, and activity. Alvyn Freed separates from intimacy a seventh category—fun. In counseling with my clients, I find "fun" a useful distinction. The specific way we structure our time determines the probability of satisfying two more primary hungers—the need for varied stimuli and the need for recognition by our fellow human beings.

Analyzing Use of Time

How do we, feeling "there are just not enough hours in a day," begin to use our time better? Many of us want to start today in planning for tomorrow. After all, procrastination is a time waster. However, behavior modifiers recognize in their technique to change habits that the first step is to assess carefully what we are doing now. Peter Drucker states that when time managers start with a plan, they usually discard these same plans before they finally organize their time. Successful time managers begin by assessing how they are currently spending their time. The first step, then, in time management is to keep some sort of record as to how you are already using your time. The way in which you decide to record your activities may range all the way from a very structured printed-form journal to a diary on a sheet of paper. The important thing is to be accurate in recording the way you use your time. In any case, it is best to keep the journal throughout the day rather than waiting to the end of the day and "remembering" how you have spent your time.

Time Wasters

The second step, once you have a record of time structuring, is to analyze the data. An important piece of information is to look for ways in which you waste your time. Ted Engstrom and Alec MacKenzie distinguish between internal and external time wasters. A partial list of these time wasters follows.

Internal time wasters include lack of setting priorities, unclear objectives, procrastination (both in making decisions and in carrying them out), lack of self-discipline, discouraging feedback, lack of energy (or fatigue), failure to delegate responsibility, depression (or other bad feeling), poor management tools, mistakes, blaming others, not listening, and inability to say no.

External time wasters include junk mail, socializing, telephone, incompetent subordinate, poor communication, questionnaires, unscheduled meetings (or too many scheduled), poor filing systems, interruptions, red tape, crisis management, fantasies (beautiful secretaries), too much reading, television (the last insert is mine). You may have others in your own time structure.

It is possible to take any one or any group of the above time wasters and make a plan to respond differently to future invitations to waste time. For example, when a telephone rings, you do not have to answer it. The world won't come to an end if that particular person does not get your attention at that time. It is okay to finish your task if that is what you have decided to do. You might decide to use some of the self-monitoring or consequential techniques mentioned in Chapter 7 to decelerate the probability of your getting into time wasters.

Time Structure

A second analysis is to decide how you structure your time by separating your time into Berne's categories. How much of your time did you spend *withdrawn* from other human contacts? Actually, you may be in the company of others but withdrawn in the sense that you are not listening to or interacting with them. A certain amount of withdrawal is certainly okay in your daily life. However, if you are feeling socially deprived or deprived of recognition from other individuals, you are not likely to get it in withdrawn activities. Withdrawing includes watching television, reading a book, working alone on a hobby, or tuning people out at a party.

What is the percentage of time during your week that you spend engaging in ritualistic activities with others? *Rituals* are socially appropriate responses that are highly predictable, such as simple greetings, table manners, proper introductions, and stereotyped social behavior. Rituals are important because you get a certain amount of recognition for "doing what is expected." However, rituals provide very low-intensity kinds of recognition and get very boring after a time.

How much of your time do you spend chitchatting, making shallow conversation around some particular topic? This time structure Berne calls *pastimes*. Pastiming helps you avoid silence when you are with other persons. The skill of chitchatting is socially necessary.

Without the ability to pass the time, you would be left with either withdrawing or getting into emotionally strong conversation with other people. Pastimes are necessary and helpful to discover those people with whom you wish to have a deeper relationship. However, pastimes become boring after awhile, and there is a need for more social stimulation.

Assess the amount of time you spent in interacting with other individuals in which you attempt to manipulate them in some way, are manipulated by them in some way, or in general exchange negative regards so that both of you end up with bad feelings. This is Berne's *game* structure. According to Berne, a psychological game is a series of complementary transactions in which there is an underhandedness or "con" element having a definite payoff (usually involving bad feelings). Psychological games produce intense emotion and therefore are very exciting and stimulating. The payoff in the game is what happens after a switch in the drama triangle explained in Chapter 7. Although games are very exciting, they are an inefficient use of time. Game playing on the job or in families creates bad feelings and generally wastes productive energy and time.

Did you have any fun during your time sample? Fun doesn't have to follow a big special event but can occur in a few minutes interacting with a friend. I don't have to tell you how much *fun* enhances the quality of life. Productivity can be realistically balanced out with fun, producing activities. In my work in industry I have noticed that executives who might be very competent and who express a sense of well-being on the job have a great deal of difficulty at the cocktail party in the evening. They seem uncomfortable and can't wait to find an excuse to go back to the office and "do more work." These individuals don't have "permission" to have fun and therefore have a lopsided life-style.

How much of your time structure do you allow for intimacy? *Intimacy* is defined by Berne as game-free interaction with another person. Intimacy is a closeness with a great deal of trust. In intimate relationships the openness usually involves some degree of vulnerability. Therefore, intimacy can be scary and threatening and may be totally avoided by some persons who fear getting hurt. Intimacy is more than a psychological state of being. It has physical characteristics, generally described as a mild euphoria. In general, intimate interactions don't take up a great deal of your time, but they are of high quality and fully as exciting and reinforcing as structuring your time games.

What is the percentage of time that you spend in productive *activity*? This activity might include planning, decision making, directing and controlling, organizing, or "doing" (working with your hands). Productive activity lends itself to a high potential for reinforcement from other people and from yourself. Some sort of activity takes up a large portion of most of our days.

Setting Priorities

Now that your time structuring has been analyzed, you are in a position to decide how you want to structure time in the future. At this point you are ready to set some goals and develop a plan for reaching those goals. Once you have a list of goals before you, the next step is to set priorities. In setting priorities it is important to eliminate low-priority tasks, which may persist because they are easier to do. This is the stuff that procrastination is made of. You may do many unnecessary but easy tasks, while avoiding the more difficult but more rewarding ones. The object is not to get more things done but to do a few things well. Alan Lakein has set forth an easy method for setting priorities. He invites you to rate your goals in terms of life goals and progressively more immediate goals which are ranked into A, B, and C priority. Lakein, in general, suggests doing the A priority goals and getting more and more comfortable with not doing the C through Z priorities.

Lakein speaks of the 80-20 rule. He states that 80 percent of the value is in the first 20 percent of work time on any given task. He advises not to shoot for perfectionism but to be certain that those tasks on which you want to expend the last 80 percent of effort are important. You don't "have to iron out the last wrinkle from the sheet, but you might check thoroughly for errors in an important business letter." He advises not to go past the point of diminishing returns.

Work Smarter

MacKenzie states, "One of the myths of time management is that the harder one works, the more he gets done. . . . No direct relationship can be assumed between hard work and positive accomplishment. The adage 'work smarter, not harder' has its root in the recognition of the fallacy of this assumption." "Work harder" generally means that you are putting a good deal of effort and energy into low-priority tasks to justify to the world how much energy you are putting into your work and also to reveal to yourself how little you are getting for your efforts. (Remember the Try Hard driver.)

Worry vs. Planning

Productive people spend a portion of their time planning. Those of us who are time wasters may spend a portion of our time worrying or getting tied up with trivia. There are those individuals who have difficulty in separating the planning and the worrying. Actually, they are quite different. Worrying is generally within the time structure of withdrawal. You are into your own thoughts and exclude what is going on around you (or are involved in a game to manipulate others). Planning is usually related to productive activity. You may be into your own thoughts, but eventually you translate your thoughts into behavior.

If you still feel that worry is necessary and helpful, I suggest that you structure time to worry, rather than allowing it to seep into your activity throughout the day. That is, you may set aside a time to hassle and worry or to consider future fantasies of disaster. When you designate a period for worry (fifteen minutes), you should do nothing but worry during that fifteen-minute period. In fact, you can increase the worry to the highest possible level so that you will "get it all out of your system." I encourage those of you who believe in worry to set aside much shorter periods for worry and hassle than you set aside for fun. That certainly makes a difference in your quality of life.

Delegation

Delegation of authority to make decisions and to carry out duties is a key time issue in any organization, be it business or family. The issue is clearer in business where good managers delegate to the lowest level capable of making the decision or carrying out an act. Delegation in a family is often not openly considered. In some families there is a rule, often unspoken, that no decision is made without the husband (or wife) being the authority. I have found husbands who complain about this role—but who demand it by discounting their wife's ability to think clearly. An extreme example came up in a marriage counseling session when the husband reported on the following conversation.

Wife on telephone: "Darling, I have a flat and I don't know what to do."

Husband: "Hell, we have an appointment at 1:00. Where are you? I'll come fix it."

Wife: "I am calling from the Esso service station on I-55."

Husband: "What! Well, why don't you tell them to fix the damn thing?"

Wife: "I thought so. I just wanted to check with you first."

Interestingly enough, when this complaining husband was invited to specify the areas in which he was willing to turn over decision making to his wife, he balked, stating that she could not think or remember at a level that would allow her to be successful. Underdelegation results in bottlenecks and overwork.

Overdelegation also takes place in families as well as in business. Overdelegators give away responsibility along with the authority to make decisions. They usually end up taking the role of blamer, criticizing others when they don't make perfect decisions. They take little responsibility themselves to assist in decision making. The result is turmoil and unhappiness in the system—a great time waster.

In summary, the basics of time management include:

1. Set daily goals.
2. Set priorities and list these priorities in a "to-do" list. Exclude or eliminate low-priority tasks, and focus energy on the "A" priorities. To do this it may be helpful to set deadlines and stick to them.
3. Identify and eliminate time wasters.
4. Delegate.
5. Reward yourself for meeting your goal.

The ultimate goal in time management is to develop good habits of time utilization. Eventually, these habits will become automatic, rather than requiring conscious effort to "make yourself do things against your will." The behavior of structuring your time may have to occur over and over again and be reinforced each time before it becomes a habit.

Chapter 9

You Don't Have to Feel Bad

Chapter 3 put in perspective your responsibility for your feelings, and Chapter 5 defined healthy and unhealthy feelings. Feelings have been pictured as both motivational and manipulative stimuli used to control others. Yet with all of the above information, you may still suffer from powerful emotions that interfere with problem solving. Emotion in this chapter is defined as an experienced feeling state along with the behavioral expression of that feeling. Uncomfortable emotions may block thinking, lead to escape problem solving, drain off energies so that you no longer care, or enrage you into using poor judgment.

Blocked feelings may cause a different set of problems. Here you may exclude signals (feelings) from your awareness and lose valuable clues to problem identification and solutions. Efficient problem solving depends on being in touch with and in charge of your emotions. Is there a contradiction in the ideas that controlled feelings are harmful but learning emotional control is necessary for good problem solvers? Not really. By emotional control I am suggesting the capacity to experience feelings fully and to change or give up those feelings that are not useful in daily living.

Overcontrol

One school of psychotherapy devotes its treatment techniques to the relationship of the body to thoughts and feelings. Bioenergetics was developed by Alexander Lowen and is an extension of Riekian therapy. The bioenergetics therapists diagnose emotional problems through visually assessing the harmony of the body. Their therapy is intended to open the body to all sorts of feeling experience and expression of feelings.

Robert D. Palmer reports on a number of studies which suggest that the emotions are directly related to body posture and facial expression: "An individual's posture and facial contraction patterns also appear to directly influence his own mood and emotional responsiveness." E. Gellhorn reports that when the posture accompanying "triumph" was "locked in" through hypnosis, a depressive mood could not be brought about until the subject's postural setting was changed. J. D. Laird manipulated subjects' faces into "smile" or "frown" expressions without their awareness of the nature of the manipulations. Consistent with the James-Lange theory of emotion, the quality of their subjective experience of emotion was related to the manipulation of expression. S. S. Tomkins has described the facial patterns associated with different feeling states—the reddened, frowning face and clinched jaw seen in states of anger. Different emotional states seem also to be associated with different patterns of physiological arousal.

Evidence presented by B. Mittelmann and H. Wolff, for example, suggests that physiological response to uninhibited aggressive use of the extremities is an abundant blood supply to the hands and feet, and that anxiety about aggression leads to the opposite pattern—vasoconstriction of the extremities.

To experience emotion fully you must exhibit the behavioral patterns associated with that emotion. Any interruption of the posture, facial expression, or physiological reaction may dilute or prevent the emotion from occurring. If you would like to test this concept out for yourself, attempt to get angry while standing on your head. This unfamiliar posture not often associated with anger makes sensing and expressing the emotion quite difficult.

Unwanted emotions can be controlled by taking shallow breaths in the upper part of the chest, tensing the stomach or other muscle groups, or exhibiting a facial expression inconsistent with the felt emotion. Bioenergetics therapists have developed a series of exercises designed to free up the emotional blocks so that you can experience and express the emotions.

A client of mine wanted to be more in touch with her emotions. She had been in group therapy for approximately one year and had achieved a great deal of success in terms of dealing with her family problems for which she sought therapy. However, she recognized that she was "less in touch with her feelings" than other people appeared to be. While observing this woman in a situation that might have produced a feeling, I observed that the muscles in the back of her neck expanded. In fact these muscles regularly expanded to some extent each time she inhaled. I had to check my own neck muscles to make sure that was not a natural response. My approach to this particular block was to attach scotch tape to the back of my client's neck. I instructed her to "learn how to breathe without expanding your neck and feeling the tape stretch." After a few minutes she was able to do this, and then she began to express rather intense emotions that were unrelated to the current situation. She also had a memory flash of her father telling her not to express her feelings.

A second way of dealing with emotional blocks is to train the individual to have an integrated bodily system of emotional expressions in all the major emotions. This training is very helpful if a videotape apparatus is available.

Emotional blockers exhibit the behaviors of the Be Strong driver (Chapter 6). A frequent report when a Be Strong individual gets into training in emotional expression is, "I feel silly doing this," even though "this" is normal emotional facial expression.

Unwanted Feelings

One of the most frequently complained of feelings in my clients has been anxiety or fear. Phobias are quite common in normal as well as clinical populations and can create a good deal of discomfort. Fearful feelings are closely followed by requests to eliminate sad and angry feelings.

The first step in eliminating undesirable feeling states is to identify any secondary gains for retaining the feeling. Secondary gains are frequently involved in feeling states seen as totally undesirable. Even if the original feeling developed without secondary gains, most feelings over time have some effect on the social environment, especially if they are translated into behavior.

A client of mine came with the expressed purpose of ridding himself of resentful feelings toward his wife. He stated that seven years previously he had heard his wife talking on the telephone to her lover. My client stated that he had carried resentment and hostility toward his wife since that time. I asked this client to argue the point that the feelings were valuable to him. At first he resisted this suggestion. However, when given permission to "make up some good reasons," he did argue the point. Through his argument, we looked together at some possible secondary gains.

In the first place, he had maintained a good deal of control over his wife by frequently bringing up her affair and inviting her to feel guilty. Because of her guilt feelings, she was always "trying to make it up to him." Why was my client coming into therapy after seven years of having an "unwanted" feeling? He was presently seeking therapy because his wife had had enough of his badgering and was currently threatening to leave him if he brought up the subject again. Although his wife was threatening divorce, she still expressed guilt over her act of seven years ago and allowed him to control her to some extent. That is, she was reinforcing his bad feelings by feeling guilty.

Secondary gains are sometimes not as easily recognized as in the above case. Often there is a good deal of resistance in the client to seeing them as secondary gains. However, it is worth pursuing possible secondary gains because the best treatment regimen is doomed to failure if the secondary gains are motivating the individual to continue his bad feelings.

Competing Responses

There are a number of techniques that set up behaviors or feeling states which compete with the undesirable feeling state. One of the classical treatments was developed by Joseph Wolpe and consists of (1) training and relaxation and (2) developing a hierarchy of fearful images. The image at the lower end of the hierarchy is vaguely related to the fearful situation and therefore only mildly arousing; the image at the opposite end of the hierarchy is the most feared stimulus. Individuals, while extremely relaxed, bring to mind images at the lower end of the hierarchy until they can call to mind the image with no discomfort whatsoever. They gradually work their way up the hierarchy until they can imagine the most feared stimulus situation and remain relaxed. At this point they are encouraged to face the actual feared object or situation in their environment.

An older but less popular way of producing competing responses is the use of hyponosis. It is possible to hypnotize individuals and have them associate a very pleasant experience with a signal they generate by touching thumb and forefinger. Individuals are given a posthypnotic suggestion to touch thumb and forefinger on the next occasion when they experience the undesirable feelings. The competing response of the pleasurable feeling is brought about by the signal of thumb and forefinger, and when successful, it will lessen the impact of environmentally produced uncomfortable feelings.

Bandler and Grinder, at a 1977 group psychotherapy workshop in New Orleans, Louisiana, report on two techniques that can be carried out by an individual without the aid of a psychotherapist, although a therapist may increase the ease of the exercises. The first technique of disassociation is described as follows.

Nurture the Uncomfortable Child in Yourself

1. Sit comfortably in a chair, and go back in time with the uncomfortable feeling that you want to change. Find a time earlier in your life when as a child you experienced a similar uncomfortable feeling.
2. Shift your thoughts to a current situation in which you feel competent and powerful and experience a sense of well-being. This can be any current real-life situation or a fantasy regarding the future. In any case, stay with the fantasy until you experience the internal sense of well-being.
3. Now, while you remain comfortable in your seat, form a visual image of you as a child across the room from where you are sitting and imagine that you have just experienced the uncomfortable feeling.
4. As you remain comfortable in your chair, disassociate a part of yourself and watch as the image of you comforts the memory of the child in a state of bad feelings. Watch as the image of you gives the child all he or she needs to restore a state of comfort and well-being. If at any time you begin to feel uncomfortable sitting in your chair, stop the image and again create your sense of well-being. When the child in your memory has all that he or she needs and feels adequate again, imagine internalizing both the image of yourself comforting the child and the child. Feel the child inside you now in a comfortable state.

You can repeat this exercise with as many different childhood situations as you wish. The value is in developing an incompatible and competing response of a sense of well-being with the undesirable feeling.

Anchoring

1. When this exercise is led by a therapist, the therapist invites you to imagine a situation that produces the undesirable feeling. While you are imagining this feeling, the therapist gently touches you on one side of your body. You may associate this touch with the uncomfortable feeling a number of times.

2. Then the therapist asks you to switch to an intensely positive experience. Remembering any situation that produces intense positive emotional feelings (for example, an orgasm) develops a powerful competing response. As you imagine the positive experience, the therapist touches you on the opposite side of the body.

3. The final step is for the therapist to give both signals of touch at the same time, thereby mixing the two feelings. Most of my clients report that at first they flip back and forth between the two feelings, but after awhile they experience the intermingling of feelings that neutralizes each one.

Thinking and Feeling

Most feelings are at least partially maintained by or associated with a thought. When you are experiencing intense feelings, you may report that you have stopped thinking altogether. What you may in fact be doing is not engaging in productive thought but dwelling on thoughts that are associated with the feelings you experience. If you can be encouraged to think thoughts other than those associated with the feelings, you may interfere with the chain of events maintaining the feeling state. You may agree that this is a good idea; however, you have found that you cannot force yourself to think because of the intensity of your feelings. However, since the feeling is prominent on your mind, you can at least think about the feeling itself.

For example, if you are experiencing intense anxiety, you can be led into giving the anxiety a physical appearance. That is, you can give it a shape, form, weight, color, and texture; and you can be encouraged to maintain the image of these physical characteristics. As an actual fact, the image will always change as the feeling itself becomes less intense. The value in this exercise is to get you to focus on a thought other than that producing the undesirable feeling. If you attempt to capture the feeling you are experiencing intellectually, the feeling will likely go away because you have changed your thought patterns.

Another related way of encouraging you to think about your feelings is to keep a log of measurements of your feeling experiences. That is, you can, with a stop watch, measure the duration of each feeling. You can measure the amplitude and frequency of a feeling for a given time period. This technique has been very successful in my working with flight phobics. People with a fear of flying can be given a thinking task to carry out on their airplane trip. The thinking interferes with the feeling, and the person has the experience of flying with much less fear.

Implosion

Implosion treatment, popularized by Stampef and called "flooding" by other writers, calls for you to keep in your mind, as long as possible, the fearful stimulus. You are encouraged to do everything in your power to increase the intensity of the uncomfortable feeling. Although you may do your best to keep the intensity high, after awhile the feeling will go away. This technique can be done alone or with a counselor.

I have had a few patients who arrived at this technique on their own. For example, I had a client who upon learning of his wife's affair experienced intense anxiety. He had partially treated himself before he came to my office by forcing himself to picture his wife with her lover and keep the image in mind until as he described it he "didn't care anymore." As he kept the mental image of her in the presence of a lesser emotional feeling, he began to extinguish his intense feeling states to that particular stimulus image.

Giving "Reality" to Thoughts

Thoughts are not "real" events and do not deserve the feeling state associated with real events. However, you may be responding to thoughts *about* doing something as if you were *going to do it*.

For example, a mother is angry with her child. She is in the kitchen and looks at a knife. She has a mental picture of stabbing her child and reacts with horror. Any of us may have an associated thought from a hierarchy of possible thoughts (associating anger at child and knife) that is in reality unrelated to our potential behavior. The mother above would not necessarily have an unconscious desire to harm her child, as she might fear.

The problem escalates as she, now horrified, shuts the thought out of her mind. She has now created the sequence: (1) evil thought, (2) panic feeling, (3) stop thought, (4) relief. This sequence is a learning sequence reinforced by the relief. The events in the sequence prior to the relief will be likely to reoccur in the future. That is, she must have the thought leading to tension and stop the thought to get the relief. An obsessive thought may have been created in which this mother now has the disturbing idea many times per day.

Treatment consists of distinguishing between thoughts and real events. Obsessive thinkers have difficulty with the distinction. The next step is to separate the emotional reaction from the thought. Clients are instructed *not* to shut off the thought. Instead, they reaffirm that the thought is just a thought and of no danger. They are further instructed to bring the thought up on purpose and consider its contents without the emotion (similar to flooding). Since the thought is no longer reinforced by leading to tension and then relief, the probability of recurring thought is decreased.

Emotional Window

Although feelings are an integral part of most of our problems, there are two purely feeling problems at opposite poles—understating or blocking feeling at one end and overstating or exaggerating feelings at the other. Feeling blocks have already been discussed.

For some of us feelings are the major guideline by

which we live. Feelings are worshiped and given a higher status than rational thought. We may admit we used poor judgment, but at the same time we justify our behavior because we "felt so strongly about it." We are responding to very low-level stimuli with emotions, and the overemotionalism interferes with problem solving.

An analogy to the amount of stimuli that are emotionally arousing is the Cyborg Window of Silence on the Cyborg SPR PSOS biofeedback equipment. The window can be opened and closed on this apparatus to allow either more or less electrical skin potential to produce auditory and/or visual feedback to the client. The window control "permits the operator gradually to shape SPR amplitude and frequency by progressively lowering (or raising) the criteria for 'acceptable' response amplitudes."

We have a differential sensitivity to stimuli, *our own emotional window*. The amount of stimuli allowable is affected by our thoughts and behaviors (postures, breathing, ideas). Since parts of the "window" can be under conscious control, once they are labeled, we can decrease the amplitude of stimuli to which we will respond or increase our response to lower amplitudes. (Most of my clinical data has been on reducing response to stimuli.)

1. Make a commitment to close (or open) your window to less (or more) stimuli.
2. Estimate your current window aperture on a 0 to 100 scale with 0 being no response to intense stimulation and 100 representing extreme response to weak stimulation.
3. With each emotional encounter, gradually (in your

thoughts) "close" (or open) your window. Experiment with different thoughts, postures, relaxation of the body, until you experience a change in your window.

4. Continue to monitor your change until the window allows stimuli at a level that helps you identify and solve problems but that is not overwhelming (or unrecognized if increasing the window apparatus).

This exercise has never resulted in a client "overdoing it." This labeling and self-monitoring is usually helpful in controlling the undesirable emotional state.

Summary

All feelings, whether comfortable or uncomfortable (other than those directly affecting us physically), are learned and therefore can be relearned with the proper technique. Controlling your emotions begins with a decision on your part to give up the bad feeling and to give up any secondary gains along with it. The next step is to repeat one of the exercises given above. I suggest that you repeat the exercise a number of times before you pass judgment on it. However, after a number of repetitions if you do not subjectively experience a reduction in your feeling state, you may call on a psychotherapist to aid you in stopping a particular uncomfortable emotional state.

Chapter 10

Assertive Behavior: Taking Action to Get Your Needs Met

In our modern world, most actions designed to satisfy some need are social actions; in complex societies, getting our needs met takes a great deal of social skill. These skills generally center around communication, either verbal or nonverbal. We must be able to let others know where we stand in regard to issues and what we want or expect from them.

All communication is designed to have some effect on another person. When we express something, either with our actions or words, we want another person to make some change either in his thinking or feeling or acting. Artistic expressions or expressions of love or sorrow may not be designed to produce any outward reaction; however, even these communications are intended to produce a feeling state—of excitement, love, or sympathy—within another.

As assertive individuals, social communication skills such as tact and diplomacy are necessary to involve other people in helping us get our needs met. Other people also have needs and want to affect our behavior, thoughts, or feelings so that we will behave in a manner compatible with their needs. Sometimes the needs of both parties are consistent, and cooperation is easy. At other times, however, needs conflict and competition exists. In competition, social skills become even more important.

To summarize, we as social beings, to get our needs met, must use skills to invite others to take certain actions consistent with our needs. When other people have needs incompatible with our own, we must decide whether to compromise or to use our skills to avoid their diverting our time and energy away from our own wants to help them satisfy theirs. The development of this area of social skills has been labeled *assertive training*.

Assertive training was popularized by the work of Joseph Wolpe and his associate Arnold Lazarus in their book *Behavior Therapy Techniques*. Since that time, some useful techniques of training have been developed from behavior therapy for the nonassertive person; for example, maintaining good eye contact, speaking clearly, and rehearsing assertive dialogue.

Persons associated with the women's movement and industry are especially interested in assertive training. Currently there are books on the subject, as well as assertive groups and workshops in larger communities. Assertive training groups generally involve teaching through modeling techniques. Another technique, video feedback, teaches consistency of assertive words, gestures, and other behavior. Correct assertive behavior is then reinforced by the trainer, and reinforcement may be set up in the environment for appropriately assertive behavior. Such training is valuable in changing behavior; however, we can progress considerably on our own in learning to take charge of our life space and assertively resist intrusion.

Assertive training, in its broadest interpretation, includes expressing our needs and wants in a fair manner without being aggressive toward others. Examples of assertive behavior include standing up for our rights without blaming or attacking others, expressing positive regard, and asking for what we want in an honest and straightforward manner that allows others to respond in an equally honest and straightforward manner. In addition, assertive behavior is a way to communicate and work together for a compromise when there is a conflict or problem.

Why Not Be Aggressive?

If getting your wants and needs met is a fundamental goal, would you not ultimately get what you want more quickly and efficiently if you learned to intimidate, coerce, and undermine those who are in a position to satisfy or frustrate your goals? Why not study aggressive techniques?

In close relationships, there can be no winner-loser dichotomy. Regardless of how strong and efficient one person seems, no matter how many times that person triumphs over another, the opportunity for "guerrilla warfare" is always present. An apparently weaker individual can create actual misery for the more aggressive "opponent." In families or other close relationships, there can be only two winners or two losers when a conflict arises. The focus of assertive training, then, is to assert your rights in such a way that you do not aggressively usurp the rights of another, so that each of you emerges from the interchange feeling okay about yourself.

How Do You Go About Getting What You Want?

Most theories of assertiveness deal with three basic responses that you may take when someone attempts to "push you around." You might respond to this pressure from others by being very passive and doing nothing actively to discourage those around you from taking charge of your responsibilities. A second possibility is that you will aggressively attempt to manipulate the other person. The third response is characterized by the term "assertive." The assertive response is the expression of your own wishes and desires without infringing on the rights of others to express and seek the fulfillment of their own wishes and desires.

Beyond the three basic responses generally treated in theories of assertiveness are two other possibilities. First is a combination of the passive and the aggressive. People clearly engage in passive-aggressive behavior when they take no direct action in response to aggressive behavior directed toward them. Passive-aggressive persons, however, are very active on an indirect level for which they avoid taking responsibility. Carl Steiner calls this kind of behavior "guerrilla warfare"—a kind of power play made from the one-down position. The one-down player typically makes no immediate response to pressure from outsiders. However, after taking a lot of "stuff" from others, the passive-aggressive individual can play stupid and make mistakes that are hurtful to the aggressor, create guilt in the aggressor, or engage in a myriad of other operations intended to frustrate the aggressive person. Examples include a wife beating her husband over the head with a credit card or the child levying heavy blows against his parents with bad grades.

Another possible attitude is defiance. Defiant individuals are willing to lose all, but they will also see that others involved get nothing. Their motto is, "You can't make me." Defiant behavior may be either active or passive.

How do you determine where you fit most of the time? The following diagnostic criteria will be helpful in deciding which of the basic roles related to power moves between individuals is most characteristic for you.

What Is Your Most Frequent Role?

Passive Role

Passive individuals characteristically will appear confused under stress. They may state, "I am confused"; they may act confused; they may speak in a confused manner; or they may do all three. They expect those around them to take responsibility for them and, in particular, to do their thinking for them. In exchange for having others take responsibility for their thinking and problem solving, passive persons in turn will attempt to please others at every opportunity. In situations that require passive persons to make decisions, they lack confidence and therefore feel compelled to check out any decision with another person. They expect failure.

Passive persons discount anger, feeling instead frustration, fear, or depression. After denying feelings of anger for a time, they may blow up and experience guilt feelings as a result. In the passive role, people are expected to endure uncomfortable temperature, offensive smoking, poor service, and other inconveniences. They tolerate discomfort because they feel that other people are okay and that they are not okay. ("Okay" as used in this book is an existential position as defined by Thomas A. Harris in his book *I'M OK, You're OK.*)

Aggressive Role

Aggressive people manipulate others to get what they want. They strongly fear loss of control and avoid situations that they feel will threaten their ability to control. They block awareness of feelings because feelings are experienced as being outside of their control. Under stress, they shift blame to other people or to circumstances. By shifting blame, they infinitely postpone accepting the responsibility for changing themselves. Aggressive people are "labelers." Once they label you, they respond to you in terms of your label rather than your behavior. For example, aggressive persons might use the diagnostic criteria given in this chapter to assign labels to those around them, rather than to perceive people more clearly as they really are—with all of their complexity. They will then use their labels to control others—"you're passive-aggressive"—meaning they don't like what you are doing.

Aggressive individuals want immediate satisfaction of their needs. Though they deny their own problems, they are usually willing to help others solve their problems. Aggressive persons manipulate others with both negative and positive control techniques. They are likely to be judgmental, sarcastic, distrustful, and angry when they experience bad feelings. When they are feeling good, they go out of their way to be nice to others and especially to play a rescue role—which involves taking responsibility for others' thinking and problem solving. In this way, they always stay in control. They see themselves as being okay and others as having problems and not being okay.

Passive-Aggressive Role

Passive-aggressive people share certain characteristics of the passive personality; however, they are usually more in touch with their own anger. Any aggression motivated by anger is indirect, and responsibility for the aggressive behavior is denied. Passive-aggressive individuals may feign confusion or refuse to listen to irritate or frustrate others. They will attempt to take up your time, to manipulate you into trying hard to make them do something. They often enjoy maneuvering two other people into an argument. They may casually—and apparently without realizing what they are doing—point out others' weaknesses. Another example of passive-agressive behavior is involving the interest and energy of another person in a project, then dropping all enthusiasm for the project. The passive-aggressive person may forget an appointment, spill a drink on important papers, or forget to pay a utility bill until the power is cut off. The existential position of the passive-aggressive person can be summarized as, "I'm not okay; you're okay, ha, ha." The "ha, ha" means, "If you wait around long enough, I'll show you how not okay you are."

Defiant Role

Defiant persons are typically those who were led to believe by their parents that perfection was a possibility, and they tried very hard to achieve that goal. After continually failing, they gave up and grew bitter, finding then a sense of power by throwing monkey-wrenches into things so that they don't work. Defiant individuals use their creative energy to figure out what people want, and then they do the opposite. Their philosophy is, "No matter what the consequences, you can't make me do . . ."

Defiant persons enjoy setting up "corner" situations in which you are "damned if you do and damned if you don't." They are angry much of the time, usually become lonely and rejected, and find themselves cornered so that they never get what they want. They believe that they are not okay, that no one else is okay, and that the entire situation is therefore hopeless.

Assertive Role

Assertive individuals are aware of their rights as human beings. They assert these rights while respecting the rights of others. They take total responsibility for their own thinking, feeling, and behavior. While they avoid taking responsibility for solving other people's problems, they are problem solvers themselves. Assertive persons openly and straightforwardly express both positive and negative opinions.

The basic existential position of assertive individuals is, "I'm okay; you're okay." When a conflict exists, their position is still "I'm okay; you're okay. However, what you're doing is not okay with me." The target, then is assertive behavior.

Why Isn't Everyone Assertive?

How do we stop ourselves? Why don't we naturally stand up for our rights in a rational and assertive manner? Aren't we biologically programmed for survival, and doesn't survival depend on our taking care of ourselves?

Biologically, the emotion of anger functions to motivate us to respond aggressively to outside aggression or competition. As our civilization developed, however, living together closely in large social groups made it necessary that aggression be controlled. As we grow older, we receive a number of instructions on how to control our desires in order not to interfere with the desires of those around us. For example, a child is not given a candy bar he asks for while shopping with his mother, so he screams and stomps his feet. Only a few months before, his crying would have resulted in his getting fed; now the same behavior is punished. As a consequence, feelings of anger that originally stimulated assertive or aggressive behaviors recall many "don't" messages, which are then followed by feelings of confusion and anxiety.

Coupled with the conflict between feelings of anger and socially acceptable behavior is the conflict that exists between messages prevalent in society. For example, we are told to be polite, not to talk back, and to show good manners. Respect and diplomacy are required. At the same time, popular television and literature demonstrate that success comes through aggression; the people on top are the ones who stepped on anyone who got in their way. The Bible says, "Turn the other cheek." An equally popular proverb reads, "Nice guys finish last." This pervasive conflicting dialogue becomes internalized.

As a result of the inconsistencies, some people choose to respond to only one message; however, they may still hear the other messages and feel conflict. Some people may "turn the other cheek" and remain passive. Others respond to the aggressive messages and push people around to get what they want. Another group is passive, "taking it and taking it" until they feel completely justified in being aggressive and striking back; that is, they obey both messages at different times. Another way to follow both sets of instructions at different times is to be selectively passive, aggressive, or assertive depending on the circumstances. A further possibility is to be passive-aggressive without taking responsibility for the aggressive intent.

With the typical models we have in everyday life, how does anyone learn to be properly assertive? Actually, most people don't. Natural assertiveness on a consistent basis is a rare quality. Most people who consider themselves assertive are in fact aggressive. Some people discover ways of being assertive through trial and error; some, by following good models. The problem with trial-and-error learning is that some people also learn passive, aggressive, and passive-aggressive approaches through their trials and errors. The problem with learning assertiveness by following a good assertive model is that there are too few good models; not everybody has a good assertive model in his or her territory. Thus, most people have some shortcomings in being assertive.

In addition, two strong cultural messages related to stereotyped sex roles must be managed to be properly assertive. Women are expected to please others; and men, to cover up their feelings. Of course, these two attitudes overlap into both sexes; however, when either one is a controlling directive of behavior, assertiveness is impossible.

Assertive Rights

The limits within which we allow ourselves to operate assertively are determined by our concept of what is right, fair, and equitable. Having an unrealistic idea of your rights may put you in a position to be manipulated by others. For an excellent discussion of assertive rights, see *When I Say No, I Feel Guilty* by Manuel Smith. Smith voices a basic right in his statement, "You have the right to be the ultimate judge of yourself."

Though much social behavior is governed by rules, there are many situations with no clear-cut rules. In such cases, those of us who are not assertive may invest in another person the right to make judgments as to the correctness of our behavior. As we give up the right to be the judge of our own behavior, we also give up the freedom to make our own choices among the possible courses of action in a situation.

When we relinquish our right to be the judge of our own behavior, we are in a position to be manipulated. For example, a manipulative person may devise a right and a wrong where no clear-cut rule exists. He may say, "You shouldn't do that; it's wrong," to get what he wants at the expense of another. A second example is the manipulative ploy of extending established rules into other areas. Such is the case when an employer attempts to extend his authority to control an employee off the job.

Rules can be broken. There are resultant consequences. Whether you choose to break a rule because you feel it is inappropriate in the situation, unfair, or for another reason, it is your right to break any rule as long as you know the consequences and are willing to be responsible for your decision. The assertive individual is able to make a choice, based on a rational judgment, whether to follow or not to follow a particular rule.

Smith lists nine more rights in "A Bill of Assertive Rights," which stem from the above basic right. You have the right to:

1. Offer no reasons or excuses for justifying your behavior.
2. Judge if you are responsible for finding solutions to other people's problems.
3. Change your mind.
4. Make mistakes and be responsible for them.
5. Say, "I don't know."
6. Be independent of the goodwill of others before coping with them.
7. Be illogical in making decisions.
8. Say, "I don't understand."
9. Say, "I don't care."

Smith further develops each of these rights in his book; however, I will comment on the one that seems most shocking to my clients—the right to be illogical in making decisions. This right is one of the most valuable in avoiding being manipulated. As Smith points out, logic is often used to prove us wrong so that we will do the manipulator's bidding. Most daily decisions are made on the basis of feelings—not logic. In other words, we do things or we don't do them on the basis of wanting to or not wanting to. We use logic to explain our actions only when we are trying to give justification to another person who *wants* something different. If logic is accepted as the criterion of who should control the decision, the best debater in a relationship always *wins*, even if the original decision was based on a "want to" rather than an "it is most logical to."

For example, a "logical" thinker prefers one movie over another. His preference is based on the fact that he likes historical movies better than comedies. His roommate, preferring the funnier, opts for the other movie. Our logical person starts in, "Of course, you realize that movie A has been mentioned for an Academy Award."

His friend is at the feeling level, "But Woody Allen is so funny."

"Yes, but I've read the top New York reviewers who say movie A will be the best movie of the year."

And so it goes. The point is that, although the logical person is arguing "logic," he is actually motivated by feeling. If he preferred comical movies, he would argue perhaps that those same reviewers had been wrong in the last several movies he had seen and therefore could not be trusted, or give some similar "logical" justification of his feelings.

Of course, logic does have a valuable place in solving daily problems. Many logical discussions lead to new information and helpful decisions. You must develop your skill of discrimination so you will know when logic is being used to justify a feeling or to impart valuable information. As an assertive person, you can exercise your right to choose how you respond to logical discussion, and you can learn when logic works for you or against you.

Assertive Techniques

Nonverbal Communication

Assertive behavior is primarily a communicative function. Communication involves much more than what we verbalize. Virginia Satir refers to metacommunication, which is the total implied message involved in any communication. We cannot talk to one another without signaling how we feel about what we are saying. Much of the metacommunication is nonverbal. Voice tone, eye contact, body posture, facial expression, and gestures can enhance, distort, or destroy the meaning of any communication.

An assertive individual maintains steady eye contact and adequate level of voice tone. Imagine asserting your rights while looking at your feet and mumbling as you shuffle around. This would signal a weakness and invite others to push you around. Eye expression is an important element of nonverbal communication. The major emotions can be expressed by changes in muscle groups in and around the eyes; fear, anger, sadness, excitement, or sexual arousal can all be communicated in this way. For example, dilation and contraction of the pupils clearly evidence emotion.

Spatial distance between individuals serves as an immediate indicator of interpersonal attitudes. For example, assertive communication is less effective if you are standing fifteen feet away from the person you're speaking to. On the other hand, being face to face and less than one foot away from the other person usually signals aggressiveness and a desire to intimidate by intruding on the space of another. A friend of mine who is an FBI agent told me of his training in the use of invading a suspect's interpersonal space; the suspect then is theoretically less able to resist interrogation.

In summary, facial expression, body posture, and gestures must all agree with the assertive verbal message, or conflicting messages may be sent. For example, a correctly assertive verbal message may have little effectiveness if you give a palms-up, helpless gesture with your head slightly lowered and your brow wrinkled. Your nonverbal messages are consistent with a plea for help, rather than a display of assertive strength.

Unexpected Response

A limitation of much instruction on assertiveness is that the impression is given that assertive responses are all rational, adult, straightforward communications. Rationally dealing with a conflict situation is certainly an important element in problem solving. However, more flexibility in diverting an argument or avoiding manipulation can often be accomplished by unexpected responses.

In communications designed to get needs met, you depend on your ability to predict the responses of another person. For example, an aggressive person might make a statement inviting argument because he feels he will win an argument in that particular situation. On the other hand, a passive person might remain silent, predicting that the person he is dealing with will take responsibility for making decisions and solving problems. An unexpected response—that is, one that is not the response predicted—anywhere in the chain of stimulus-response interaction will disrupt manipulation.

As a more concrete example, consider the instance of an aggressive domineering person who intends to express displeasure to a colleague to produce guilt. He angrily points out a mistake that his colleague actually did make. He is probably expecting either an argument or an apology. If his colleague argues with him, the aggressive person predicts that he can not only prove his colleague wrong but also produce bad feelings such as guilt. If his colleague apologizes and admits guilt from the beginning, the aggressor has immediately met both of the objectives. An unexpected response would be for the colleague to comment on the aggressor's perceptiveness in catching the error. To continue with a few sentences of genuine praise and perhaps appreciation for the reminder of an error and to evidence no guilt whatsoever would be a totally unexpected and assertive response.

In the above example, the assertive person makes use of information without feeling unnecessary guilt about having made an error. It is important to remember that negative intentions such as those of the aggressor are generally out of awareness; however, much of social interaction is actually structured to produce negative feelings. (See Eric Berne's *Games People Play* for a cogent discussion.)

Unexpected responses break up manipulation so that the real problems can be dealt with and bad feelings can be avoided. In Transactional Analysis, this blocking of aggression outlined above is called crossing transactions. A crossed transaction is an unexpected response that blocks communication or changes the focus of the communication to another direction. For example, if one person asks the time of day from a second person who is wearing a watch, and the second person answers by giving him the correct time, the transaction is complementary and there is understanding. Communication is not blocked, and the direction is not changed. One is expected to give the time of day when asked to do so. However, if the second person answers by criticizing, "You never know what time it is," communication is blocked. The response is unexpected and may shift the focus from getting information to arguing. (Of course, this example of a crossed transaction would be unhealthy, aggressive, and not assertive.)

The rule is that, if you like the tone of a conversation and wish it to continue, use a complementary expected response. However, if you don't like what is being said and wish to break up the pattern of communication, cross the transaction with an unexpected response. Unexpected responses may involve rational, parental, childlike, humorous, or any other unpredictable stratagem.

Attitude

Before you begin your assertive methods of communication, your effectiveness can be enhanced by your attitude toward yourself and the person you're talking to. When you feel okay about yourself and also okay about the other person, even though he may be attacking you, your approach will be positive and goal oriented rather than defensive.

To maintain mutual okayness you must stay out of the persecutor role. Any attempt to punish the object of your assertiveness will increase the probability of retaliation. Rescuing others or playing victim are other roles that lead to not okay feelings about yourself and others. If you become aware that any of your behavior falls within any of these three roles, you can stop them before continuing your assertiveness.

A third area that may interfere with assertive techniques before you begin is either exaggerating or underestimating your own power. Likewise, underestimating or exaggerating the power of others decreases the probability of effective assertiveness. An attitude that is realistic and concerned with mutual respect will increase the success of your assertive behavior.

Personal Criticism

Personal criticism is one of the most difficult human communications that you must deal with. Negative information about yourself usually brings up old childhood memories, such as times when your parents corrected your behavior and invited you to feel not okay. Even though criticism is valuable in helping you grow personally, your first reaction is likely to be defensive. You may completely overlook the value and usefulness of the information and feel hurt or resentful.

Others generally criticize you from a parental position and may feel, modeling their own parents, that you should feel bad, as well as get feedback on your behavior.

As an assertive individual, you can separate the useful information from the punishing criticism. The first procedure is to get the critical person calmed down so that he is giving information without the punishment. Several of Steve Karpman's crossed transactions, from his 1971 article, may be used as unexpected responses, thereby blocking the criticism. Once the put-down conversation is stopped, you may then ask for the useful feedback.

For example, George says to Robert, "You don't have the brains God gave an ant. You're stupid!"

What are Robert's options? If he is unaware of assertive skills, he can go to his childhood defensive feelings and behavior (to which ego state the criticism was aimed) and say, "That's not true. If your damned instructions had been more clear in the first place, I would not have made the mistake." Or he may agree with George and state, "You're right. I always do everything wrong."

With either of these childish (defensive or guilty) responses from Robert, George is likely to escalate his attack.

Robert has the option of changing to a parental response himself. However, his parenting can be nurturing, loving, warm, and understanding. Several of these nurturing examples follow; however, if any of these do not fit your personality, make up some that sound more like the loving "parent" in you.

> "Gee, George, you must have had a tough day. Why don't you sit down and relax. I'll get you something to drink."
>
> or
>
> "I wish you wouldn't do that to yourself. Getting upset only increases your blood pressure."
>
> or
>
> "We are too good friends to say hurtful things."
>
> or

"We are not setting a good example for our fellow employees."

or

"Why don't you take the day off, you know how much fun you have on the golf course."

A second alternative is for Robert to stay in his child but appeal to the warm part of George's parent instead of the critical aspects.

"What you're doing to me is really not being help-ful, and I know you care."

Robert, in his child feeling state, can get excited in a positive way and either extend positive regard to his friend George or appeal to his humor.

"Hey, I like your new tie, where did you get it?"

or

"Wow, I admire your energy. You really put a lot of feeling into what you're telling me."

or

"Of all the stupid people in the world, I'll bet I am in the top 2 percent."

or

(With legs pressed tightly together) "Wouldn't you just know it, at an important time like this I have to go to the bathroom."

Only the most persistent criticizers will follow you in-to the bathroom.

After any of the above ploys to get George off his back, Robert should go back and find out specifically why George is angry and decide whether a correction on his part is in order.

Get Your Attacker to Think Rationally

When we get into criticizing others, the behaviors we call upon are modeled after a criticizing parent. The behaviors are automatic with little rational thinking involved. The focus is more to punish than to give information. Not all criticism is of this sort; but if we are into angry feelings, we are not thinking clearly or rationally.

As an assertive person, you want to invite the other person to think rationally so that the communication may be rational. Any stimulus that requires computing, thinking, or "figuring out" will do. Asking the critical person to add a column of figures or to remember what he had for breakfast two days before will invite him to think; however, such statements are hard to work into a conversation. If Robert asks, "What time is it?" or asks George to repeat what he just said—"I didn't quite hear that, George. What was that about an ant's brain?"— George has to think about his response. He has to check his watch or remember what he has just said and report this information. Both responses require rational thinking.

A second maneuver is to go off on a tangent, such as Robert saying, "Stupid—that reminds me of this monkey I saw at the zoo. You know, that monkey acted like a guy I knew in the second grade. Boy was he stupid." George has to get into his "thinker" to figure out what Robert is talking about.

Another ploy is to bounce a response off a third party: "Jim, did you hear what George just said to me?" George has to listen in thoughtfully to make sure Robert is not distorting facts.

Finally, a nonrational person is forced either to "think" or to be confused by the use of big words. Unfamiliar words are always good attention getters:

"Stop *objurgating* my actions."
                    or
"Our problem is *ephemeral*."
(This term usually gets attention because of its similarity in sound to a sexual deviation.)
                    or
"Please don't *anathematize* my mistakes."

Even if the critical person knows the meaning of these words, their use is infrequent and he will have to search his memory for their meaning. Look through the dictionary and pick out a few attention-getting big words that will fit for you.

All of these responses that invite George to think in a rational manner should be followed by a rational, adult problem-solving response from Robert. In fact, all of the above "unexpected" response options should be followed by solving the problem that originated the transaction in the first place. Some rational problem-solving statements are as follows:

"Sounds like you have some important information for me."
                    or
"Let's check out your facts."
                    or
"What do you suggest now?"
                    or
"Yes, you're right. It was stupid and I won't do it again."

Many times the critical person has a right to be correcting you but has no right to be angry and punishing. Here you force the aggressor to take responsibility for his anger or give it up. I personally had an experience of being attacked for a real reason, but the feeling tone was out of proportion to the problem. I asked the person if he was really as angry about the situation as he seemed by his behavior. My attacker immediately denied any anger (which would have been inappropriate) and discussed the problem in a more reasonable manner.

Another way to deal with an aggressor who is not being straight is to respond to what he says rather than to what you and he both know he means but is unwilling to take responsibility for. For example, when a person is pouting (a communication that something is wrong) and he is asked what the trouble is, the pouter usually answer haughtily, "Nothing's wrong." He wants you to spend some time and effort to find out what the problem really is.

You may respond to what the pouter says by answering, "Oh, I am glad nothing is wrong. I have had a great day myself. Let's do something fun."

The pouter is then in the position of backing up his statement that nothing is wrong or, more likely, being straight and telling what's bugging him. Either way you avoid being forced into figuring out what's wrong and allowing the pouter to manipulate by not being straight.

Ideally, the above options are used to get the aggressor out of his punishing position without putting him down, while letting him know that he has been heard so that problem solving is in process.

Aggressive Manipulators

You don't have to be "right." One way aggressive people manipulate is through your belief that you have to be logical and right (usually by their definition) in what you do. As Claude Steiner puts it, "If you can't prove it [your right to do it], you can't do it."

Manipulators are usually good debaters. If others can outtalk you and you can't prove your point, you may give up going after what you want. Giving yourself permission not to have to prove you are right will result in a new freedom to be assertive in getting what you want. Oh, you may say, that sounds immoral. There must be guidelines to what you're entitled to have. A "rightness" helps you set those limits. This is the kind of thinking the manipulator wishes you to have. Your right to be illogical has already been "logically" established earlier in this chapter.

Smith in his book on saying no has an excellent technique of allowing the other person to be "right" and still get what you want. The technique is called *fogging*. Fogging "teaches acceptance of manipulative criticism by calmly acknowledging to your critic the probability that there may be some truth in what he says, yet allows you to remain your own judge of what you do."

An excellent opportunity to use fogging is when a salesman is prepared to sell you something you don't want, by having a well-prepared answer for each of your objections. The secret is, don't object! Agree with everything he says and calmly, in the face of all his logic to buy, maintain your *right* not to buy.

Fred says to Stewart, "Your committee should choose an indoor office party this year instead of a picnic. You know some of us will get bitten by bugs."

"You're probably right, Fred. However, I am voting for the picnic."

"Stewart, do you realize the high incidence of sunburn this time of year? A sunburned employee might miss three days of work."

"You make good sense, Fred, but I am sold on the picnic."

Should Stewart choose to argue with a point made by Fred, then his choice of the picnic is dependent on his ability to defend logically his choice. You are on the spot because of a belief that you must prove the "rightness" of what you want.

Being Assertive with Someone You Love

People who you love and who love you can behave in ways that are displeasing. Because you spend most of your free time with people you care about, there are more opportunities for differences of opinions. Intimacy with someone assumes that openness and honesty is a part of the relationship.

The object of communication in an intimate relationship is to inform without manipulating and to give others an opportunity to change what they are doing in light of new information about how you feel. Jean Maxwell in the pamphlet *OK Childing and Parenting* gives an excellent formula for such communication from which the following statements below were derived:

"I feel (*insert your feeling*)
When you (*insert their behavior*).
What I want you to do is (*insert the changes you wish them to make*)."

For example, a client's husband had an annoying habit of bringing home dinner guests unannounced. She confronted him in the following manner:

"I feel angry when you bring home your friends and business associates without asking me first. What I would like is for you to inform me at least before noon that day so I can get prepared."

The request was reasonable, and he agreed without being threatened. Should she, instead, have berated him and brought up all the times in the past he had "pulled this on her," he would probably have gotten defensive and lashed back. At the very least, he would have felt bad unnecessarily.

A second example, one related more to business than to personal closeness, came from a client who received "too much supervision." She worked for a government office that always had a backlog of work. Her supervisor would call her on the interoffice phone many times per day for insignificant reasons (in my client's estimation anyway) and frequently looked over my client's shoulder. This particular supervisor took a month's vacation, and my client's production increased by one-third. These data were a clear indication of the supervision interfering rather than augmenting her work. A week after her supervisor returned, the old problem reappeared.

Ms. "Client" approached the supervisor, after a video practice session, with the following:

"I feel frustrated when you call me and talk to me so much that it interferes with my work. I wish you would save your feedback until the end of the day unless it is an emergency."

Her supervisor looked stunned and irritated but complied the next day. My client followed up the third day with:

"I am really pleased that I have a supervisor who listens to me. You didn't interfere a single time yesterday. So many of my friends complain that their supervisors don't listen."

Her supervisor's new behavior remains to date.

Helpless Manipulators

In conflict there is often a rush to "prove" who has been victimized the most so they may control through guilt. Helpless people first make you responsible for solving their problem and then do nothing to problem solve themselves, or in some cases they make it even more difficult for you to solve their problems just to experience the power in frustrating you. Helpless persons may expend just as much creative energy in getting you to solve their problem as you put forth yourself in solving it for them. They learn the skill of getting others to do their thinking for them, and they have a false belief that this is the most efficient way to get their needs met.

The first assertive decision is not to take responsibility for solving other people's problems when they can do it themselves. For example, my eleven-year-old son entered from the backyard one Saturday afternoon stating, "I'm so bored, Daddy. What can I do that's fun?" My first impulse was to come up with all the fun things one can do on a sunny Saturday afternoon. However, my advice would have been things that appeared to be fun from my adult perspective. He probably would have argued with each suggestion (based on past experience). My answer was, "David, that sounds like a real problem to me. I sure hope you figure something out."

"Don't you know anything I can do?" he continued.

"No, but I sure hope you think of something."

Ten minutes later he was playing ball with a friend.

A favorite technique of helpless people is to get you to give them advice and then find fault with your advice. (They can always find something wrong with good advice.) Eric Berne called this maneuver a "Yes But" game. If you do decide to give advice and each time a flaw is pointed out, simply stop the advice giving and wish them well in solving their problem.

Helpless people take the child-victim position and invite you to be their parent, either persecuting and telling them to shape up or rescuing and doing their work for them. As I said, they invite you to take the top-dog position, but they cannot force you to do it. You can be childlike or play the victim role. Sometimes this maneuver is faster than dealing with them in a rational manner.

If a client comes into my office crying helplessly and refusing to work on his problem, I sometimes reach in my drawer, pull out a balloon, and begin blowing it up (a technique suggested by Curtis Steele) or go to a corner of the office and stand on my head. The client usually gets parental and persecuting himself, "What in the world are you doing?"

"Why, I am standing on my head."

"That's ridiculous. I have a problem to work on."

"Yes, you're right," I say, returning to my chair. "Let's work on your problem."

Sometimes the switch gets him to take more problem-solving responsibility. When it doesn't, I go back to my child or listen but give no advice. I have never lost a client by this unusual behavior.

Helpless manipulators are masters at not answering questions, avoiding saying no directly, making excuses, copping out on commitments in avoiding responsibility. In dealing with such evasive techniques, you must be persistent. The broken record technique mentioned in Stanlee Phelps and Nancy Austin's *The Assertive Woman* and M. J. Smith's *When I Say No, I Feel Guilty* is effective in such cases.

For example, talking to a furniture salesman, "If I buy this chair, can you deliver it on Friday?"

"I will try my best to have it delivered."

"Is that a yes answer?"

"I'll do what I can. I sure do want to give you good service."

"What will it take for you to know for sure?"

"I'll have to check with our driver, but I think he is booked up Friday."

"Is that a no then?"

"Well, no, we really can't get it to you until next week."

Helpless people will give up their helpless role and be responsible if you are persistent.

Asserting the Positive

Expression of positive regard for yourself and others is an important assertive action. Before positive expression takes place, you must train yourself to identify, recognize, and maintain awareness of things you appreciate in others' behavior and wish them to continue. Unrecognized behavior may not be repeated. "I like the way you" may reward and therefore maintain a desirable act. Expecting a colleague to continue doing something because he "should know it is appreciated" may not work.

The expression of positive regard is one of the strongest possible teaching techniques. New skills are more likely to be acquired and old behaviors maintained with positive expression of appreciation and recognition. The most valuable technique in training supervisors is teaching them how to use positive regard or reinforcement to motivate and maintain behavior.

Another important reason for making an effort to recognize and reinforce desirable behaviors is that people will not coexist in the same environment and remain ignored. As human beings we demand to be noticed. However, the attention and regard we get from others need not be positive. If no positive recognition is forthcoming, a person will settle for, even force, negative attention. We have more control over a decision not to give the positive than over not giving negative. Even a small child can escalate his aversive behavior until he forces a negative response. Since some kind of response will be elicited, we can take the initiative and make sure to deliver whatever positive regard is called for by noticing the other person's behavior.

If you yourself do not receive a positive response from others, if your good deeds go unrecognized, you will have a difficult time remaining assertive. The likelihood is that in time you will set up negative situations rather than remain ignored. Likewise, it is important to "take" positive recognition when it is offered by others. To discount compliments is similar, in the end, as not to receive them at all. A person who discounts the positive will set up manipulations that result in a negative interchange. If you fully absorb a compliment, you will know because it "feels good." Saying "thank you" to a compliment may not mean you take it fully. You may still block the internally reinforcing feeling.

As an assertive person, you are ready to receive and accept compliments; however, you maintain the right to be selective. You need not take compliments for behaviors you are deciding to change. For example, if a friend tells you he liked the way you "told off" that waiter who was giving poor service (and you were aggressive), you may say to him, "Thank you, but I am in the process of changing my aggressive behavior, and I don't want compliments for doing it wrong."

A second reason for not taking positive regard (at least not at the feeling level) is when you suspect that the complimenter is either being manipulative or insincere. You need not be taken into a manipulation just because the other person is being nice and complimentary.

If you feel deprived of notice, recognition, or appreciation, it is your responsibility to get what you need. It is nonassertive to wait on someone else to notice and compliment. It is okay to ask for the positive regard you want. There is a strong cultural injunction against asking for what you want. In fact, many people feel that if you ask first and then get the recognition you want, it doesn't count or feel good. This is a weak position, leaving all the initiative to other people. You can ask, and you can also be perceptive enough to know if the other person is being straight with you.

Finally, you will recognize your own accomplish-

ments and give yourself "pats on the back," compliments, and deserved praise. You will recognize your
shortcomings, but you will not dwell on them. To remain assertive you must maintain the existential position of being okay with yourself.

Limitations of Assertive Training

My experience in training people to become assertive has led to the observation of several pitfalls in post-
training results. People who have been passive most of
their lives become elated when they find that people do
listen to them when they assert their rights. They realize that they can actually get more of what they want by
asking for it. Their excitement sometimes turns into
pushy aggressiveness. They are pushy about an insignificant matter, which a person more comfortable with
his or her assertive skills would overlook. Some of this
behavior is trial-and-error learning expected from a
novice with any new skill. However, awareness of the
possibility of "overdoing it" is a useful safeguard.

At other times assertive novices learning unexpected, humorous crossing of transactions become sarcastic. Their humor is cutting and invites resentment.
I personally made the above mistake. I felt that I was
being verbally witty when I was being offensive. Fortunately, I was given appropriate feedback before much
damage was done. It is valuable to have assertive friends
who are willing to give this feedback.

In some business or legal situations in which you
have "rights" but lack the power to avoid punishment
for being assertive, it is better to remain silent. Assertive responses, no matter how well performed, don't

always work. Assertiveness increases the probability of success in getting your needs and wants met; there is no guarantee of success. It is okay to recognize these circumstances, do nothing that might increase the discomfort you are experiencing, and get out of the situation as soon as possible.

At times the assertive responses outlined in this chapter, even when correctly carried out, do not work. You are encouraged to use your own creativity rather than give up, especially if the situation is one that cannot be escaped in a relatively short period of time.

A client worked for a very critical boss. Her mother had also been critical of her as she grew up. The combination of her history and the persistent behavior of her boss resulted in frequent anger and crying at work. She planned several assertive responses that did not work. Her boss was firm in his old habits. He simply didn't listen to her crossed transactions and maintained his critical stance. She planned a new approach.

One afternoon she asked her boss to stay a few minutes after work to talk to her. She believed she had a better chance of holding his attention after working hours. She stated her desire to share a very personal problem with him. She told him of her overly critical mother and how, as a child, she developed a severe case of diarrhea in response to her mother's criticism. The case was so serious that medication gave no relief. Further, this old condition was now returning. Sometimes as a child she would spend long periods of time in the bathroom and be very weak afterward. She then asked her boss to write her a short memo when he had critical feedback for her instead of verbally "jumping on her" like her mother did. He reluctantly agreed.

Of course, her boss's old habit would occasionally crop up again in the form of a verbal attack. She would immediately head for the "john." His slipups became less frequent and less vehement. On one occasion he hurried out of his office, following her down the hall and promising to have the agreed-upon memo on her desk as soon as she returned.

How Do You Start to Be Assertive?

You have read this chapter on assertiveness. Some of the ideas make sense and you are interested, but there are no assertive workshops for you to attend. Can you start on your own from what you know? Here are some suggestions on how to begin.

The beginning of assertive behavior starts with a decision that you will be assertive because you have a right to be and because you see the benefit of standing up for your right. If you have a long history of being passive, the above decision may be easily reversed if your first assertive actions are not successful.

The following steps are a good beginning:

1. *Get into your okay feelings.* This is the hardest part. Skill is required to feel okay about yourself and the other person. You may want to review early chapters relating to this skill.
2. *Memorize two or three options to cross undesirable transactions.* It is best to choose those that best fit your personality. Make up your own.
3. *Choose a single situation in which you wish to start.* Most people can predict a future situation in which assertiveness will be required. It is a good idea to rehearse what you expect to happen and several possible responses. You can get two chairs and

switch back and forth playing both roles or ask a friend to rehearse with you. Looking in a mirror also helps to see if your nonverbal behaviors are consistent with your words.

Chapter 11

Putting It All Together: Solution Training

Solution training is the structured approach to psychotherapy and consultation in which the trainee is systematically guided to identify blocks in problem solving, to generate alternative action, and to implement workable solutions. The solution trainer directs the trainee to remain active in the problem-solving process and to avoid getting stuck in a passive position.

Solution training involves ten steps through which the problem solver moves to deal with potential blocks in achieving a solution. The trainee's response to each step suggests specific therapeutic remedies constructed to aid in getting back to successful problem solving. Solution training is designed to use the trainee's immediate problems as a vehicle to train him or her in problem-solving procedures. The eventual expected outcome is that the trainee will take responsibility for being his or her own agent of change, his or her own psychotherapist.

Solution training is taught by the use of three chairs.

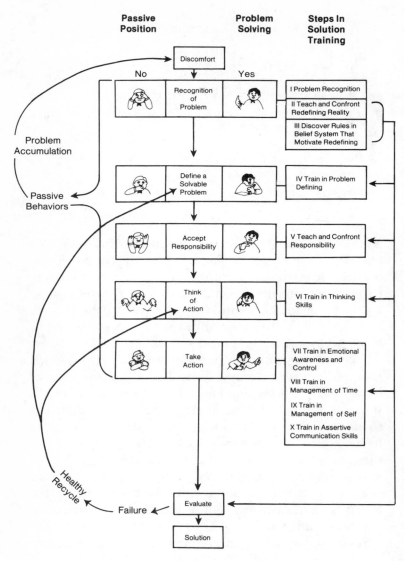

Figure 5
STEPS IN SOLUTION TRAINING

The trainee sits in one chair and faces an empty chair. One chair is the problem-presenter chair, and the other is the problem-solver chair—"problem chair" and "solver chair" respectively. The trainee switches back and forth between the chairs. In the "problem chair," he or she presents the problem, identifies the basic needs or discomfort, sets change goals, defines the problem clearly, and follows the other problem-solving procedures to take direct action in solving the problem. The "problem chair" reflects the trainee's current level of problem-solving skills.

New trainees are on a continuum of poor problem solvers to relatively good problem solvers. However, all of the trainees need assistance early in their process of learning. The "solver chair" is used by the trainee to correct mistakes in procedures and to reinforce correct problem-solving technique. This two-chair technique externalizes (for the trainer to observe) the usual "talking to oneself" that the trainee carries out in his or her head.

The trainer sits in the third chair and is the consultant to the "solver chair." The novice (solver) will not have information to give to the "problem chair" without help from the consultant-trainer. The trainer withdraws more and more and gives added responsibility to the trainee. The trainee is judged a good problem solver when he or she can clearly follow all of the steps in a solution training model. The exercise is considered complete when a particular problem has been worked through and the format may be repeated with new problems, with less input from the trainer.

If the trainee gets "stuck," the trainer may "model" by moving back and forth between the "problem" and "solver" chairs, modeling correct problem-solving procedures. Another option if the trainee remains stuck (usually a trainee assuming a very helpless, passive approach) is for the trainer to use the two chairs to "discuss with himself" his problems in training the passive trainee. The trainer ends up with a positive new action to take with the trainee. The trainee sits in the consultant chair and observes. He or she also consults with the trainer's "problem-solver" chair with information about what will and will not "work" in personal motivation.

For example, Mr. Ashley is ready to define a problem that he will be trained to solve. I explain to him what the chairs represent and ask him to follow the problem-defining steps as outlined on a blackboard.

Problem Chair: "My discomfort is that my supervisor doesn't consult with me about problems in my department until he has discussed them with other people. He makes up his mind what I am to do, and then he calls me in and tells me to do it."

Solver Chair: (Mr. Ashley moves to the solver chair, grins, and looks at the trainer for help.)

Consultant Chair: "Did you get a clear picture of the situation creating discomfort from the problem chair?"

Mr. Ashley: "Yeah."

Consultant Chair: "Good. Give yourself a pat on the back. Tell your problem point of view that he did a good job; then go for the next step."

Solver Chair: "You did that well, Bill. Now, how do you want things to be when you have solved your problem?"

Problem Chair: "I want him to consult me at the first opportunity after he hears about the problem."

Solver Chair: "That's good."

Consultant Chair: "Find out what basic need you're satisfying with this goal. Look at the list on the board."

Solver Chair: "What need are you satisfying?"

Problem Chair: "Self-esteem on my job."

Consultant Chair: "The way you have defined your goal—is it the best way to solve your need for self-esteem? Invite yourself to check out other goals."

Solver Chair: "Is your goal the best way to get your basic need met?"

Problem Chair: "Yeah, that's what I want to happen."

Consultant Chair: "Information for you: goals that are totally dependent on somebody else's behavior are risky. However, let's go ahead and see how it comes out."

Solver Chair: "Define your problem so that it points to an action that you can take."

Problem Chair: "My problem is that my supervisor has no confidence in me."

Solver Chair: "Okay, how are you going to take action on that?"

Problem Chair: "I need to get him to have more respect for me."

Consultant Chair: "Hold on. Before you consider possible solutions, let's look at the definition. A problem defined must have a probability of being solved and point to an action that the person owning the problem can take. The supervisor's perception of you is important. However, your problem must be defined so that it points to a specific action that you can take."

Solver Chair: "Let me see . . . Define it like the Doc says."

Consultant Chair: "Bill, since this is a training session, you will learn more if you will go ahead and state your instructions to yourself."

Solver Chair: "Define your problem so that the solution doesn't depend on your boss and so that the definition points to an action you can take."

Consultant Chair: "Good, that was very clear."

Problem Chair: "My problem is I do not communicate my desires, feelings, or goals to my boss. My problem is communicating what I want directly to my boss."

Mr. Ashley generated several alternative actions and in the process found that he had some experiential blocks that kept him from taking action. He had a skill deficit in assertive communication.

The ten solution training steps are presented in detail in the rest of this chapter. They are written for psychotherapists or counselors training their clients. However, these steps are also applicable to you as an individual working independently. If you get stuck in your independent development, it is okay to consult with a professional counselor.

Step I
Recognizing the Problem

Problem recognition involves confronting clients with the information that they are in a state of discomfort and in a passive position. That is, they are not engaging in thought or actions designed to relieve the discomfort. It also involves identifying the unfulfilled need or want producing the discomfort.

Instructions. Give the solver chair a list of passive behaviors (Exercise A), and instruct your client to have a discussion with the problem chair regarding existing passive behaviors.

Exercise A
Passive Behaviors

(The levels are related to the degree of distress experienced as the problems accumulate. The distress is related to the number of stimuli in the immediate experience capable of evoking a bad feeling.)

Level I *Feel better without solving the problem.*

A. Do nothing about your problem and instead
1. Hope
2. Daydream
3. Blame others
4. Focus on someone else's goal for you. Get others to decide what is best for you. (Disregard your own wants and needs.)
   a. Help others by doing what they want you to do.
   b. Rebel and keep others from their goal (for you).

Level II *Feeling dominates thinking*.

1. You feel agitated, antsy, and you may tap your fingers or feet, pace the floor, wring your hands, or some other non-goal directed behavior to release the tension.
2. You may act on impulse, using poor judgment.
3. You may repeat a behavior that isn't working for you because "I don't know what else to do" or "It's the right thing to do."
4. You may use alcohol or drugs to stop the bad feeling.
5. You may "lose control" and "blow up" at someone.
6. You may be confused and state, "I can't think."
7. You may worry and suffer.
8. Your behavior may result in others asking you, "What's wrong?" and "You look upset; can I do something for you?"

Level III *Force others to take care of you*.

  A. Incapacitation
   1. Refuse to get out of bed.
   2. Use alcohol and drugs to the extent that normal functioning stops.
   3. Have a "nervous breakdown."
   4. Become physically exhausted.
   5. Attempt suicide.
   6. Have conversion symptoms (body won't function in some way) or psychosomatic illness.
   7. Communicate hopelessness and despair.
  B. Become violent.

Once your client is aware of his discomfort and has identified himself in a passive behavior, he knows a problem exists and is now ready to look for an unmet need or want.

Instructions. Give your client a written hierarchy of

needs (Exercise B). Have him discuss how he is meeting and not meeting needs at each level. In the consultant chair listen for redefining, rules from the belief system, and trigger phrases.

Exercise B
Basic Needs
1. *Biological needs.* The need for food, water, air, sex, moderate temperature, and sensory stimulation.
2. *Safety.* The need to be free of fear.
3. *Social.* A need to interact with other human beings. A need to structure your time to maximize the opportunity to obtain and give recognition and to avoid boredom.
4. *Self-esteem.* A need for self-respect and pride.
5. *Self-actualization.* A need to achieve your potential.

It is helpful for the client to consider some specific means to achieve his basic needs.

Exercise C
Setting Life Goals
Lead your client through this exercise without the two chairs.
1. Sit or lie down comfortably and develop a fantasy of what you would like to be doing five years from now. Fantasize yourself on a job, at home, during recreation. What will you have to change about your present life-style to be where you want to be in five years?
2. Rank the following life goals in order of their importance to you:
   a. To be very wealthy; to acquire money and property over your life span.

    b. To become well-known in your group, community, nation.

    c. To be known as a great friend.

    d. To establish a loving relationship in which you give and receive affection.

    e. To grow interpersonally toward a self-actualized life pattern.

    f. To become powerful and to be able to control the feelings and behaviors of others.

    g. To travel widely.

    h. To serve other people; to give your time to helping others.

    i. To rear a happy family.

    j. To establish a safe, secure position rather than taking risks for higher gains.

    k. To get fun and pleasure out of life; to enjoy life.

    l. To become a major influence in your job, community, professional organization; to be a leader.

    m. To be considered an expert in your profession, hobby.

    n. To dedicate yourself to the fulfillment of your duty; to do what you are supposed to do.

    o. To be independent; to be free to make your own choices.

    p. Make up a final life goal and insert it in the ranking with those above.

In ranking you may find that some of your goals overlap and emerge into one goal. However, these goals are designed as guidelines, not as mutually exclusive categories.

    Instructions. Now move your client back into his

two-chair position. Instruct the solver chair and problem chair to discuss the ranking of the above life goals.
Next get the problem chair to estimate the percentage
of time that your client spends each week in achieving
each one of the above life goals. Instruct the solver
chair to look for discrepancies between the importance
of rankings and the time spent on each goal. You want
the solver chair to figure out creative ways to lessen the
discrepancy between the goals and the time spent
achieving the goal. As a final step invite the solver and
problem chairs to interact so that they end up with specific action which will be taken within the next seven
days related to the top priority in the goal ranking.

Instructions. One of the most frequent unmet social
needs experienced by my clients has been a deficit in
their giving or receiving of recognition (strokes). Get
your client into the two-chair situation and instruct him
to interview his problem chair to get the following
information:

1. List the kinds of attention, recognition, compliments, or criticism you most frequently give to
   others.
2. List the kinds of attention, recognition, compliments, or criticisms you most frequently want from
   others.
3. Discuss the kinds of attention, recognition, compliments, or criticisms you most frequently get from
   others.

The trainer can be helpful by writing this list on the
blackboard or on a piece of paper. The solver chair is
next instructed to look for discrepancies and points of
change for which he can direct some action.

Instructions. A second way of assessing recognition

deficits is to have the problem chair rank the following from one to seven—one being the most difficult behavior for your client and seven being the easiest.
1. Giving compliments
2. Giving criticism
3. Taking compliments
4. Taking criticism
5. Asking for the kind of attention you want
6. Patting yourself on the back
7. Recognizing your own faults

Take the top ranking and develop a remedy for the above difficulty. Since your client may have difficulties in all these areas, a strategy for the other difficulties and recognition could be developed now or at a later time.

Step II
Redefining Reality

The redefinition of a reality situation is the first clue that a basic belief of your client has been threatened. Redefining reality protects what she believes so that the belief will not have to be changed.

Instructions. Teach your client in the solver chair how to recognize discounts (indications that he is redefining some aspect of himself, others, or situations). Particular areas that are likely to be discounted are: receiving recognition from someone else, personal power of self or others, or personal worth of self or others. A reality distortion occurs when your client exaggerates or diminishes either the power or personal worth of himself or other people. Remember from

Chapter 4 that clients discount to lessen or diminish in some manner what is being discussed.

Instructions. Instruct your client in the solver chair to be very sensitive to the problem chair *not answering questions*. These partial answers are very subtle; the question seems to be "almost answered" and the questioner assumes that he has been fully answered. On one occasion I remember asking a client of mine in a group therapy situation if she would be willing to change her decision about asking other people for what she wants from them. The client answered, "I have already changed that right here in the group." At first I assumed that my client had answered my question and went on with the group process. Later I returned to the client and asked the question again. The client first stated that she had already given me an answer. I pushed for a yes or no answer, and as it turned out, the client finally returned a no. She was not willing to change where it counts, in her home situation. She had not intentionally set out to fool me but had fooled herself in an effort to avoid making a frightening change in her relationship with her family. The skill of being aware of and confronting unanswered questions is one that your client in the solver chair will pick up rather quickly, both in dealing with himself in the problem chair and in dealing with others.

Instructions. The next technique to detecting redefinitions of reality usually requires the assistance of the trainer from the consultant chair. The client is instructed to give a video camera description of the situation creating the distress. The video camera includes things that can be photographed and sounds. Listening from the consultant chair, look for elements left out of the description. This is best done with the trainer closing his eyes, visually picturing details mentioned, and pinpointing those left out. For example, the client may leave out the significant individual's facial expression. Points left out in the description often lead to *deleted* information, which is overlooked in the service of defending beliefs. The value of this technique is that a client may be "creating a problem that does not exist." He may be, in the service of his belief system, "interpreting" meaning to the situation described. The interpretation may be unusual, signifying a defense of his own beliefs.

Instructions. Instruct your client in the solver chair to look for generalizations from earlier experiences. These may be assumed when the client in the problem chair describes a reaction of his own that is not in keeping with the current situation described. At this point from the solver chair the client can interview for similar instances in his history from which he might be generalizing. Locating these historical events leads to Step III of identifying rules in the belief system that aid the generalization.

A second instance of generalization that the solver chair can be sensitive to is instances of faulty logic; for example, the logical sequence: John is bad. John is a man. Therefore men are bad. This statement is an oversimplification of the same logical sequences that clients might hide in a more complex verbal statement. Any prejudicial statement that includes all men, all women, or all of any other particular group is suggestive of generalization.

Instructions. Instruct your client to discuss from the solver chair possible discounts occurring within himself. Exercise D is modified from the Schiff discounting chart.

Exercise D
Identifying Discounts

1. If in the problem chair you are not aware of what is causing you discomfort, you are likely discounting the existence of relevant stimuli related to this problem (your own emotions, facial expressions of others, etc.).
2. If you are aware of the stimuli but do not identify a problem for yourself, you are likely discounting the significance of the stimuli situation. ("Sure, I'm angry, but so what? Everybody gets angry.")
3. You may be aware of the stimuli and also know that the situation is significant; however, you may discount the possibility of changing the relevant stimuli. ("My husband will never change and I will never leave him, so I might as well try and forget about inattention.") You are aware that a problem exists, but it is not a significant problem for you since you doubt any possibility of change.
4. You may be aware of the stimuli and the problem and know that the situation is changeable for others; however, you may doubt your own ability to bring about the desired change. ("I was rejected by my mother when I was two years old; with that early trauma, I know I can't change my attitude toward women.") You will not identify your problem as solvable for yourself, so the options that exist for others are not significant to you.

Instructions. If your client's interaction between the solver and problem chairs locates areas of discounting, he can proceed to Step III and discover the belief system motivating such discounting.

Step III
Belief System Blocks

In preparation for your client to discover various aspects of his belief system, have him complete the following assessment exercises.

Exercise E
Driver Assessment

Rate each of the following answers with the appropriate number: 0=not like me, 1=sometimes like me, 2=often like me, 3=most like me. Each question may have one and only one #3 rating.

1. *I expect others to:*
    a. strive for perfection
    b. put up a front
    c. please me
    d. do it faster
    e. try hard
2. *My voice is often:*
    a. a monotone
    b. well modulated and demanding
    c. full of peaks and valleys
    d. labored with "aaa" or pauses
    e. impatient, fast-clipped, pressured
3. *I believe:*
    a. life is a struggle requiring a great deal of effort
    b. I am responsible for making others around me feel good
    c. the more others know about me the bigger the risk

    d. if I could just go faster I'll be okay

    e. big words communicate better than small ones

4. *I am:*

    a. stoic and don't show my feelings

    b. one who covers all the bases in a decision

    c. one who often repeats the question before it is answered

    d. a watch watcher—time is all important

    e. usually checking it out with others to see how I'm doing

5. *I like:*

    a. to do things as fast as possible to get them over with

    b. to be liked by almost everyone

    c. never to let it show when I feel down

    d. for others to make an effort and fuss over me to get me going

    e. to correct mistakes made by others

6. *I don't like:*

    a. even the slightest disorder

    b. having to wait on someone else

    c. being pressured to set definite goals

    d. to ask others for help

    e. people refusing to give me what I want

7. *I would more likely be observed:*

    a. counting on my fingers

    b. with my arms crossed

    c. tapping my fingers

    d. moving my fist

    e. nodding my head in agreement

8. *My facial expression is often:*

    a. stone-faced, expressionless

    b. quick, moving eyes

    c. severe

    d. puzzled

    e. raised eyebrows

9. *I may use the expression:*

    a. "I don't care about . . . "

    b. "We have to hurry . . . "

    c. "Of course, obviously . . . "

    d. "It's difficult . . . "

    e. "You know . . . " (at the end of a statement)

10. *My attitude is:*

    a. passive-aggressive

    b. submissive and seductive

    c. worried but commanding

    d. indifferent

    e. intellectual-dominant

Score your responses to the driver questionnaire using this guide.

Be Perfect	*Hurry Up*	*Be Strong*	*Please Me*	*Try Hard*
1a ___	1d ___	1b ___	1c ___	1e ___
2b ___	2e ___	2a ___	2c ___	2d ___
3e ___	3d ___	3c ___	3b ___	3a ___
4b ___	4e ___	4a ___	4d ___	4c ___
5e ___	5a ___	5c ___	5b ___	5d ___
6a ___	6b ___	6d ___	6e ___	6c ___
7a ___	7c ___	7b ___	7e ___	7d ___
8c ___	8b ___	8a ___	8e ___	8d ___
9c ___	9b ___	9a ___	9e ___	9d ___
10e ___	10c ___	10d ___	10b ___	10a ___

Total

Exercise F
Life-Style Questionnaire

Rate the following answers with the appropriate number: 0=not like me, 1=sometimes like me, 2=often like me, 3=most like me. Each answer must have one and only one #3 rating.

1. I value:
   a. action, getting things done now
   b. ideas, innovation, concepts, theory, and long-range planning
   c. human interaction
   d. logic and systematic inquiry
2. You are more likely to find me:
   a. experiencing through what can be touched, seen, or heard
   b. putting things in logical order
   c. combining discord and elements into ideas
   d. understanding experience through emotional reaction
3. I consider myself:
   a. an "idea person"
   b. a "people person"
   c. a "thinker," clear and logical
   d. a "pragmatist"
4. I usually function as:
   a. a person sensitive to the needs of others
   b. a person who depends on rational principles, avoiding emotionalism
   c. a person with good vision, able to see relationships others do not understand
   d. a "doer"
5. Others describe me as:

    a. frequently bringing up fresh and novel approaches and ideas

    b. objective and cool in my approach

    c. decisive, a quick decision maker

    d. able to interpret behavior and sort out complex emotional situations

6. Sometimes I can:

    a. organize myself and others to research an idea and make detailed plans

    b. cut through the smoke screen of tradition and focus on the crux of the situation

    c. work tirelessly beyond my expected duties

    d. get others to cooperate and give a team effort

7. I make mistakes because I:

    a. am too overly cautious and conservative

    b. choose "gut feelings over logic"

    c. am long on vision and short on action

    d. fail to consider long-range consequences

8. Under stress I become:

    a. detached and overintellectual

    b. defensive, overreactive to different opinions and am likely to ride roughshod over the feelings of others

    c. rigid, insecure, have to be right, won't take risks

    d. subjective and impulsive, overreactive

9. I am:

    a. looking at the future with little interest in the past

    b. methodically and consistently relating the present course of action to both past and future time frames

    c. dependent on my past experience to create meaning for the present

    d. a here-and-now person living each day to its fullest, with little interest in worrying about the past or predicting the future

10. I place a premium on communications:
    a. that are well thought out, emphasizing a central thought, not wasting time on detail
    b. that sound like they are coming from a fellow human being rather than a machine
    c. that are well organized, systematic, and logical
    d. that are specific, pragmatic, and point to an action

11. In conflict with others I am:
    a. rigid and uncompromising
    b. seen as having "tunnel vision"
    c. disinterested in the feelings of others
    d. thin-skinned and easily hurt

12. Under pressure I:
    a. am subjective
    b. am uncompromising and sometimes impractical
    c. blame others
    d. am indecisive

13. I approach a difficult situation by:
    a. expecting others to agree with me if they are my friends
    b. mood fluctuations
    c. considering "ivory tower" theories instead of carefully considering the reality of the situation
    d. becoming mechanistic and impersonal

Score your responses to the life-style questionnaire using these guides.

Normal Conditions

Theorist	Thinker	Feeler	Pragmatist
1b ____	1d ____	1c ____	1a ____
2c ____	2b ____	2d ____	2a ____
3a ____	3c ____	3b ____	3d ____
4c ____	4b ____	4a ____	4d ____
5a ____	5b ____	5d ____	5c ____
6b ____	6a ____	6d ____	6c ____
7c ____	7a ____	7b ____	7d ____
9a ____	9b ____	9c ____	9d ____
10a ____	10c ____	10b ____	10d ____

Total

Stress

Theorist	Thinker	Feeler	Pragmatist
8a ____	8c ____	8d ____	8b ____
11a ____	11c ____	11d ____	11b ____
12b ____	12d ____	12a ____	12c ____
13c ____	13d ____	13b ____	13a ____

Total

Exercise G
Rules and Your Belief System

Write your response to the questions below.

1. Develop the fantasy first of one of your parents,

and then the other, giving you advice related to the problem you are solving.

   a. What are their rules?

   b. Is there any difference in how they would handle the problem personally and how they would advise you?

2. What are your real childhood memories, even vaguely related to the problem you are facing? What decisions did you make?

3. In fantasy develop a character the exact opposite of yourself. Make a list of descriptive statements or characteristic adjectives about yourself. List an opposite for each statement or adjective. Now think, feel, and behave as your opposite. Have your opposite character deal with the problem.

   a. Does he or she solve the problem?

   b. If so, what rules of yours did he or she break?

4. Develop a fantasy in which you solve the problem "no matter what."

   a. What rules of yours did you break?

   b. How did you stop yourself from thinking of these options before?

5. Complete three sentences related to your problem and begin each sentence with one of the following words: should, always, and never.

6. Which of the above rules that interfere with your problem solving would you be willing to give up?

Exercise H
Fantasies to Assess Beliefs About Yourself

1. Have a fantasy that you're lying in your crib just home from the hospital, and both parents are

standing above looking down at you. What are
their thoughts as they look at you as a newborn?

2. Decide on the five most significant people in your
life before age ten. Have a fantasy of these five
people sitting in a circle discussing their description of your character. Make sure that each individual gets a chance to express his or her own
opinion of you. In the case of a difference of opinion, you can fantasize two individuals arguing their
different points of view. Write down the major
points that each important person develops.

3. Sit in the solver chair and interview both of your
parents, asking questions about yourself. In the
problem chair role play both of your parents. If
you get "stuck" by unknown answers, "make something up."

Instructions. Have your client in the solver chair discuss with himself the life-style that he is using to solve
his current problem. Use the life-style questionnaire
(Exercise F) to identify his most frequent life-style
approach.

Have your client decide if his chosen life-style is the
most appropriate one for this particular problem. If it
is not, have him make a plan to use characteristics from
another life-style to get his needs met.

Exercise I
Stopping the Drivers

It is important that you learn to control the driver
attitudes and behaviors that precipitate bad feelings. A
procedure for driver control is outlined as follows:

1. Stop any behavior, words, postures, facial expressions listed in Chapter 6.
2. Change your driver attitude by changing the statement you say to yourself about how to be worthwhile (allow statements listed below).
3. Change your behavior so that it is incompatible with the driver behavior.

The specific changes needed for each individual driver are outlined below as follows:

Be Perfect

Allower Self-Statements

1. It's okay to be yourself. There is nothing else you can be at any given moment except what you are.
2. It's okay to be human and make mistakes.
3. It's okay for others to be human and make mistakes.
4. It's okay to give and accept positive regard even though you and others fall short of perfection.

Incompatible Behaviors

1. Look for the positive rather than what can be criticized.
2. Give frequent positive regard. Make a contract with yourself to increase the number of positive strokes given each day for one week. Monitor your progress.
3. Talk straight. Don't qualify. Use simple, everyday words and short sentences.
4. Enjoy each success, however small.

Hurry Up
Allower Self-Statements

1. It's okay to take your time.
2. It's okay to stay relaxed. You don't have to be anxious before getting things done. You don't need pressure to function.
3. It's okay to enjoy the here and now experience.
4. It's okay to avoid trivia.

Incompatible Behaviors

1. Progressively relax each muscle in your body every day.
2. Speak slowly and make fluid movements; don't agitate.
3. Stay in the present. Complete what you are doing before thinking of a new task to be done next.
4. Don't interrupt others; listen attentively.

Be Strong
Allower Self-Statements

1. It's okay to be open with your thoughts and feelings.
2. It's okay to feel whatever you feel.
3. It's okay to take care of yourself.
4. It's okay not to always be in control of situations.
5. It's okay to ask for help when you need it.

Incompatible Behaviors

1. Call attention to yourself.
   a. Do something silly.
   b. Go to a movie before the first feature. Sit down

front and stand up, pretending to wave at
   someone in back.
 c. Say the numbers out loud for each floor while
    on an elevator, or face the wrong way on the
    elevator.
2. Get in touch with your feelings through body
   awareness.
3. Be committed to issues and make your commitments known to others.

Try Hard
Allower Self-Statements

1. It's okay to take things one at a time.
2. It's okay to make it, to be successful.
3. It's okay to go ahead and do it now.
4. It's okay to think clearly.

Incompatible Behaviors

1. Keep a "to-do list" and set priorities.
2. Stay on track in conversations; develop each idea
   to a conclusion.
3. Make "will" commitments.

Please Me
Allower Self-Statements

1. It's okay to please yourself, to take care of your
   own needs.
2. It's okay to avoid responsibility for pleasing others.

Incompatible Behaviors

1. Only be nice when you really want to. You needn't
   be rude, but don't go out of your way to be nice.

2. Ask other people for what you want.
3. Be assertive.

Instructions. Utilizing the material in Exercise I, instruct your client in the solver chair to work out a specific design and plan with the problem chair to confront his most frequent drivers to lessen their frequency.

Instructions. Guide your client in identifying significant trigger phrases associated with the rules he has discovered. Sometimes these trigger phrases can only be identified in a "homework" format. The client is instructed on the next occasion when he experiences a feeling or engages in a behavior he has already associated with the rule he desires to change. He checks out his thoughts and internal statements occurring with the behavior or feeling. This situation can be simulated in the training session by having your client imagine or reproduce the circumstances in his mind and tell you what he thinks about or what phrases go through his mind under these conditions.

Once a trigger phrase is established, have your client develop a sequence of further thoughts, feelings, or behaviors as they occur following the trigger phrase. When the sequence has been established, instruct your client to work in the two-chair mode and come up with an alternative sequence of thoughts, feelings, and behaviors that are incompatible and therefore compete with his previous habit sequence. Make sure that he ends this sequence with some kind of reward for himself. Get a commitment from your client to switch consciously to the new sequence upon awareness of the old trigger phrase or any link in the old sequence.

Instructions. Ask your client to state all of the rules

that he has discovered in his belief system currently interfering with his problem solving. For each rule have your client identify the way he redefines reality to defend that rule. Have your client identify the significant trigger phrases that support the rule. Have your client write down each rule on a separate 3 × 5 card, as well as the redefinitions and trigger phrases associated with the rule. Instruct your client to refer to these cards frequently until he is thoroughly familiar with each rule and the rule-associated elements. He may increase the probability of reviewing the rules by attaching the reviewing to some daily event, such as referring to the cards at breakfast, each time he goes to the bathroom, or when he gets to the office.

Step IV
Defining the Problem

Defining a problem in a solvable manner includes the steps outlined below. These steps are put on a blackboard or communicated to the solver chair by the trainer in the consultant chair. The solver is trained to monitor her own problem-defining behaviors in the problem chair so that she ends by defining a problem in such a way that an action can be taken.

1. Have your client in the solver chair interview himself in the problem chair about the general circumstances surrounding his problem. Assuming that your client has completed Step I (Recognizing the Problem), he should have access to this information.

2. Instruct your client in the solver chair to find out specifically how he wants the situation to be differ-

ent when the problem is solved. He monitors this goal setting carried out by himself in the problem chair until he is satisfied and you are satisfied as a consultant that the goals are clear and realistic. At this step the solver chair is to invite the problem chair to review the hierarchy of basic needs. In goal setting it is helpful to recognize the basic needs being satisfied and to decide if the goals stated are the best way to satisfy those needs.

3. As a final step in defining the problem, the client takes into account the information generated in the two steps above and sets several subgoals designed to resolve the discomfort and to reach the goals set above. Each subgoal must point to or allow an action to be taken. The subgoals are small steps toward your overall goals and several are usually required.

4. Instruct your client to redefine the problem in another way. Although the first definition may solve his problem, it is important to train your client in the possibility, sometimes the necessity, of defining the problem in several different ways.

Step V
Responsibility

Responsibility is a necessary element in each of the steps in problem solving. Responsibility generally occurs at one or more of the following points:

1. Owning the problem
2. Assuming responsibility for your own feelings and avoiding taking responsibility for someone else's feelings

3. Being responsible to make decisions and to take actions based on those decisions

Instructions. Instruct your client to have a two-chair discussion regarding the ownership of the problem at hand. Inform the solver chair that anytime there is a personal discomfort the individual experiencing the discomfort owns at least a part of the problem. This includes discomfort invited by another's behavior. That is, the problem's ownership is related to a felt discomfort rather than somebody's behavior. Have the solver in the problem chair discuss the four false beliefs about responsibility:
1. You can make me feel bad.
2. Other people can make me feel good.
3. I can make other people feel good.
4. I can make other people feel bad.

In this discussion have the problem chair identify his favorite false belief and rank all the beliefs from most favored to least favored.

Instructions. Instruct your solver chair to think up a strategy for avoiding your client's most frequent or strongest false belief. One strategy is to identify the drama triangle position most frequently associated with the false beliefs (see Chapter 7).

An individual believing that other people can make him either bad or good is likely to spend much of his time and interpersonal relationships operating from the victim position. An individual who believes that he can make other people feel bad is likely to take the persecutor position. An individual who believes that he can make other people feel good will spend time in the rescuer position. After the favorite position has been

determined, the individual may do one or more of the
following:
1. Record the frequency of observed actions from
   your favorite position.
2. Enlist the aid of individuals around you to give
   feedback when they observe you in the position
   that you want to change.
3. Contract with those around you to inform you of
   behaviors from your favorite position, for which
   you would pay them one dollar (or some agreed-
   upon amount) for this information.

Step VI
Thinking Skills

Generating alternative actions emphasizes the point
to your trainee that, just as more than one definition is
possible in a problem circumstance, there are many
possible actions to solve the problem for any of those
definitions. The trainee is encouraged to think of several possible actions rather than just one and to choose
the most probable action to check out first.

The most powerful confrontation in training for
thinking skills is to inform the trainee in the solver
chair to remind himself in the problem chair *that it is
okay to "make up an answer"* when he does not readily
think of an answer. This confrontation was discussed
in Chapter 5. As noted there, the process of making
up something is the same as thinking of something.
The important difference is that the labeling to "make
it up" is a permission to brainstorm without coming up

with a good response. The individual can later evaluate the usefulness of what he comes up with.

This confrontation will probably be taught to the trainee long before this step is reached. Many people block themselves during the first interview, and it's okay to use a confrontation as early as needed. When a trainee confronts the task of thinking of workable alternative actions, a more structured brainstorming approach is useful. Brainstorming is an exercise of creative thinking in which all ideas are recorded without judging their usefulness until a later time.

Exercise J
Brainstorming

1. Use a tape recorder or write all your ideas without critical evaluation.
2. With your problem as a stimulus, brainstorm. Make the exercise fun, get wild, get ridiculous, use humor.
3. Don't stop too soon; go for quantity, not quality. Don't worry about periods of silence. Set a time goal so that you can stick with it until the time period is over.
4. Improve on the idea you have produced by evaluating each idea with the following questions. (This part of the exercise is carried out in the two-chair format with the solver chair presenting the suggestions listed below one at a time for the problem chair to use in his brainstorming.)
   a. Can you combine any of your ideas with any other ideas?

    b. What other ideas does this idea suggest? Is it almost like anything else that could be copied?

    c. Does your past experience offer any parallels?

    d. Could you modify your idea or give it a new twist? Could you change the meaning, emotion, sound, odor, form, shape, any other changes?

    e. Can you magnify your idea? What can you add? More time? Greater frequency? Make it stronger, higher, longer, thicker, of extra value, add an ingredient? Are there other ways that you can duplicate, multiply, or magnify?

    f. Can you minify your idea? Or can you subtract? Can you make it smaller, condense it, make it slower, lower, lighter, omit, streamline, split up, or understate?

    g. Can you substitute another person, ingredient, material, process, power, place, approach, tone of voice?

    h. Can you rearrange, interchange components, use other patterns, other layouts, other sequences, transpose cause and effect, change place or schedule?

    i. Can you reverse the idea, transpose positive and negative, use opposites, turn it backward or upside down, reverse roles, turn the tables, or perhaps turn the other cheek?

Instructions. Instruct your trainee to combine all of the generated alternative actions and place them in a hierarchy with the number 1 action being the one judged as the most probable of producing success.

When the brainstorming fails to yield constructive actions to take, a more intense training in creative thinking may help the individual think of new alternatives. Creative thinking involves a series of instructions designed to lead the thinker away from his current logical system. The structure allows the individual to think of ideas that lead him in a different direction from the original problem. The last step, of course, depends upon his ability to find a way to integrate this diversion thinking back into actions to solve the problem.

Exercise K
Creative Thinking

Give your trainee in the solver chair these instructions in creative thinking one at a time, and he will in turn instruct himself in the problem chair to develop his creative thinking ability.

1. Think of an example related to your goal or problem from the world of one of the following: animals, nature, physics, mythology, movies, machines, chemistry, or any other world familiar to you.
2. Direct the problem chair to develop and examine the analogies generated "from other worlds."
3. Instruct the problem chair to "become the analogy" and develop a personal experience.
4. Instruct the problem chair to think of a book title that captures the essence of the analogy. Usually the title should contain two words (an adverb and a noun), one paradoxical to the other ("Gentle Rowdiness," "Unstable Strength").
5. Think of another example from "the world of . . ." related to the book title.
6. Consider the information generated by the exer-

cise and fit your analogies to your problem situation. Incorporate new alternative actions into your hierarchy of actions previously developed.

Step VII
Emotional Awareness and Emotional Control

It is not always an accurate assumption that individuals complaining of uncomfortable emotions are fully committed to ridding themselves of those same emotions. These individuals, although they complain of the discomfort, may be getting secondary gains from these bad feelings. That is, the feelings may be in some way controlling other persons with whom they are closely associated. Bad feelings may invite others to take care of them or to get involved in their needs. Also these seemingly unwanted feelings may "make somebody else feel bad too," and the individuals' perceptions of the situation can therefore be used as a club to punish others. The following exercise may be taught to your trainee to check for possible secondary gains.

Exercise L
Secondary Gains

1. In the solver chair give the following instructions to yourself in the problem chair: "Think of all the good, valid reasons you have for keeping your bad feelings. Write down the reasons."
2. Your response from the problem chair may be, "There are no good reasons; if there were, I

wouldn't be working on the problem in the first place." Desires about feelings are complex because you can approach a problem with mixed motivations. You may have information that you "should change uncomfortable feelings." Since they do produce discomfort, you want to rid yourself of them. However, because of the secondary payoffs, you may find ways to hold onto the feelings. If in the problem chair you use some blocking explanation, instruct the solver chair to counter with the instruction, "Make up some good reasons."

3. Once some reasons are established, even though you may not identify with these reasons, in the solver chair give the following instruction: "Given that there is some possibility of truth in some of your reasons for keeping the bad feelings, how would you creatively mess up your problem solving so that you can continue to feel bad and yet appear to be trying to rid yourself of the feeling?"

4. Encourage yourself in the solver chair to push for as many ways to "mess up" the problem solving as possible. Once you have expressed a way to mess up your commitment to change, it is more difficult for you to use that same method to avoid your commitment. Give up the bad feelings and devise a strategy to deal with the self-defeating moves that you have outlined.

Exercise M
Nurturing and Competing Responses

This exercise comes from a 1977 workshop in New Orleans, Louisiana, conducted by Albert Bandler and

John Grinder. The essence of the exercise is for the trainee to maintain a comfortable and relaxed feeling in an observer role while watching an image of himself as a child who has just gone through a traumatic experience related to his current problems. Whatever your client is experiencing now and whatever the feelings, he probably had a similar occurrence at an earlier age. Take your client through the following experiences:

1. Using your current uncomfortable feeling as a guideline, think back to a previous similar situation. Picture yourself at that age standing in front of you, across the room.

2. As you keep that image in mind, get very comfortable with yourself. You can create that comfort by thinking of a situation in which you feel the most competent, are relaxed, and have a sense of well-being and self-worth.

3. Now, with you feeling secure where you are and picturing yourself at a younger age, distressed, imagine an image of yourself splitting off and going into the child image, nurturing and comforting that child. Make sure that you maintain your sense of well-being in the chair where you sit. If you begin to feel uncomfortable, stop the image in front of you and recreate the comfort. Give the "little you" all the comfort he or she needs. You may imagine holding or hugging, reassuring, or any other technique to create comfort.

4. When the younger you is fully comforted, integrate this image back into your body. This is a symbolic step. Most people report that they "feel

better" after they have integrated the comforted memory back into themselves.

In essence this technique creates a competing response in which the trainee is led through an experience that has been uncomfortable for him in the past, while remaining very comfortable in the observance of that experience. The client's negative feeling should weaken with each session, as described above. This exercise is better carried out with the trainer leading the trainee, rather than the trainee working from the two-chair setup.

Exercise N
Capturing Uncomfortable Feelings

This exercise is also better if the trainer takes a leadership role. I first encountered this technique in Gestalt and Transactional Analysis training groups.

The focus of this technique is to help the trainee get into the feeling, rather than away from it. He shouldn't attempt to escape from the discomfort. Instead, instruct your client to:

1. Measure the feeling's intensity (estimate on a 1–100 scale), duration, strength.
2. Picture the feeling in your mind's eye. Don't lose it even for a second.
3. Give the feeling a shape, weight, color, texture.
4. Keep mentally reviewing the characteristics you have given the feeling.

Within a few minutes the feeling will have abated and perhaps gone away altogether. The feeling generally changes in its characteristics as your client continues to observe it in his mind's eye. Feelings are maintained by thoughts as a part of the stimulus situation. If an individual concentrates on the feeling, he will be unable to consider at the same time the disturbing thoughts that are maintaining some portion of the uncomfortable feeling.

Exercise O
Desensitization

This classic technique for emotional control was popularized by behavior therapists for emotional control of fear and is the most frequently and widely used of the techniques.

Help your trainee develop a hierarchy of stimuli related to his uncomfortable feeling. The hierarchy should include the most terrifying thought he can imagine related to the uncomfortable feeling (usually a feeling of anxiety) and a feeling so miniscule that it is only slightly related to the uncomfortable stimuli.

Next, teach your trainee a relaxation technique. If you are unfamiliar with the deep muscle relaxation techniques, there are many audiotapes available (such as Arnold Lazarus, *Relaxation Exercises for Daily Living*, IDI, 166 E. Superior St., Chicago, Ill. 60611).

Once your trainee experiences a state of deep muscle relaxation, help him fantasize the least disturbing stimuli until the fantasy produces no unwanted feelings. Have the trainee signal you by raising a finger when he feels any discomfort. Once the last item on the hierarchy produces no noticeable feeling, move up to the next stimulus on the hierarchy and so forth until the most frightening item can be confronted in comfort.

The next step is to seek out a real-life situation that

evokes the unwanted feelings. If your trainee can face this real-life situation with relative comfort, you can judge the exercise a success. You may need to repeat all of the above several times before you get the desired result.

Exercise P
Anchoring

Anchoring is the second technique from the Bandler and Grinder 1977 workshop. Anchoring signals competing emotions that occur at the same time and neutralize each other. This exercise is also carried out with the therapist and trainee, rather than with the two-chair method.

1. Imagine a scene that produces the uncomfortable and unwanted emotion. Exaggerate the feeling as much as possible. When you have an identifiable unpleasantness accompanying your fantasy, signal the trainer by raising the first finger on your left hand. The trainer follows the signal by touching your left hand and maintaining a pressure for a few seconds. As the trainer releases the pressure, you should relax and let the scene fade away. This procedure is repeated five times.

2. Think of the most intense, pleasant experience that you can bring to mind. Involve all of your senses in that fantasy world, and give the trainer a signal when you have an identifiable pleasant feeling. You can signal the trainer by raising the first finger of your right hand. The trainer touches that hand and maintains the pressure for a few seconds. This exercise is repeated for five times.

3. The trainer gives you both signals at the same time

by touching both of your hands. The trainer maintains the pressure on both hands until you report
a neutralizing feeling.
4. Imagine the original scene, which previously produced the uncomfortable feeling. If the feeling returns full strength, repeat the entire exercise until
it is no longer needed.

Exercise Q
Feelings Resulting from Obsessive Thoughts

A special case of controlling feelings that result from
obsessive thinking occurs when individuals have a disturbing thought about which they generate an extremely uncomfortable feeling and then approach this
problem by shutting off the thought. They experience
a temporary relief. The problem is that they have developed a learning sequence in which the thought now
becomes an original stimulus for starting a chain of
events resulting in an eventual feeling of relief. The
relief is often not only from the feelings generated by
the thought, but a feeling of total relief (although temporary) from all of the problems of the day. So to get
the relief, the unwanted thought continues to return
creating a bad feeling but leading to relief.

This sequence is a difficult one to stop. One of the
traditional interventions is a thought-stopping method,
which only aggravates the situation since the individual
is stopping the thoughts (at least temporarily) himself.
A more efficient technique is set up through the two-
chair method. The solver chair initiates a discussion
with the problem chair relative to the reality of the
thought. My experience with obsessive thinkers is that
they are not likely to carry out their feared fantasies.

However, they are reacting to the thoughts *as if they were reality*, as if there were really a potential of the fear happening ("I may harm my child").

Have the solver chair give permission to the problem chair to remain calm with the thought still in mind. The problem chair is instructed to bring the thought to mind and to have an additional recognition that the thought is okay because it is only a thought and not reality. The solver chair can embellish on this procedure by inviting the problem chair to conjure up other "horrible" thoughts and learn that no actual harm occurs accompanying the thinking. When the trainee in the problem chair reports that the thought is present without the accompanying uncomfortable feeling, have him move back to the solver chair and congratulate himself and perhaps develop some sort of tangible reward for a job well done.

Exercise R
Emotional Awareness

A different kind of feeling problem involves the inability to be aware of feelings. Feelings are valuable data in the problem-solving process, and those individuals who exclude or distort their feeling experience lose that advantage in solving problems.

The two-chair procedure is helpful. Individuals who have a lot of experience in shutting off feelings are reluctant to get involved in feeling experiences. Have your trainee "argue" with himself in the two-chair exercise with the goal of figuring out creative ways to get himself to take a risk.

In the two-chair exercise, have the solver chair do the exercises related to the Be Strong driver in Exercise I.

The Be Strong driver is usually involved when feeling experience is blocked. Basically, these in-session exercises invite the trainee to give himself the freedom to be silly or call attention to himself. Also get a commitment for some of the homework exercises listed.

A second important exercise (and this works much better with videotape) is to get the individual in the problem chair to express his major feeling states including mad, sad, afraid, excited, loving, seductive, shy. In each of these feeling states he demonstrates facial expression, eye messages, loudness, voice tone, verbal content, posture, and gestures appropriate to each feeling state. It is useful to provide the trainee with a mirror and an audiotape recorder for feedback purposes and much better if a videotape recorder is available. It is important that all of the feeling expresssions are distinguishable from each other.

In my experience, a most effective way of opening individuals up to feeling experience when they are blocked is a series of exercises known as bioenergetics. These exercises are fully explained in the following book:

Bioenergetics, by Dr. Alexander Lowen

Step VIII
Time Management

Time management begins with an assessment of how your trainee is currently spending his waking hours. Time management is a skill that can be taught to all clients, even if they don't identify management of time as a major problem.

1. Begin the process by asking your trainee to keep a diary for at least one week before you begin the planning phase of time management. Have the solver chair help your trainee in the problem chair analyze his diary for potential time wasters. As you remember from the chapter on time management, there are two classes of time wasters—the internal time waster (procrastination, failure to delegate authority, bad feelings, blaming) and the external time waster (telephone, red tape, unplanned meetings). Once the time wasters are identified, instruct your trainee to develop a counterprocedure for each time waster.

2. Have the solver and problem chairs together make a list of daily goals and establish priorities. Instruct the solver chair in assisting the problem chair to exclude the lower priorities. Make sure that the problem chair has made a commitment to hold off the lower priority until that higher priority has been achieved. If there is a "need" to complete a lower priority first, the priorities have been improperly set.

3. Describe to your trainee in the solver chair the "80–20 rule" mentioned in Chapter 8. Have him discuss with the problem chair those items on the list that are to be "well done" and those that can be safely "loosely done." Remind him that the object is to work "smarter not harder." The 80–20 rule states that 80 percent of the value of a task is completed in the first 20 percent of the effort. Decide on those tasks that are worthy of another 80 percent of the effort to achieve the remaining 20 percent of the value.

4. During the next training session (usually one week after the initial discussion of the diary), check your trainee's ability to follow the priorities that he has set. If he is not following the priorities—that is, doing lower priorities and putting off the ones identified as the most important—have the solver chair instruct the problem chair to record the procrastinations. The trainee should record each time he decides to do a top priority and does anything else instead. Once a baseline record is established, he is then to commit himself to reduce the procrastinations by at least one procrastination per day. He may make a more involved commitment, such as reducing about five or ten procrastinations per day, if the procrastination rate is very high.

5. Instruct your trainee in the two-chair situation to have a discussion designed to find ways to make the task on his "to-do list" more fun and rewarding, rather than a "have-to-do list," which he experiences as drudgery. Instruct him to find ways to make each step on the list fun, pleasant, and rewarding or to follow a difficult priority with a manufactured reinforcement, such as a pleasant fantasy, an ice-cream cone, a coffee break.

Step IX
Self-Management

For a meaningful life experience it is important that we keep our commitments to ourselves and other people. The fact that a commitment is needed suggests that our current habits or ways of behaving are not working to get our needs met. Self-management involves controlling or changing an existing pattern of behavior or habit. The change generally involves delaying short, immediate, but small payoffs to get larger but longer range benefits.

1. Get your trainee in the solver chair to instruct himself in the problem chair to clearly specify and label the thought, behavior, or feeling that he desires to change. The six-chair exercise suggested in Chapter 7 is a useful technique when the particular item to be changed is not clear and the problem chair reports that his life is not working for him.

2. Have your trainee in the solver chair interview the problem chair for potential "stoppers" of the desired change. Teach the solver chair to monitor the commitments made in the problem chair and train himself to make a clear and definite commitment to change.

3. Have your trainee in the problem chair write a contract relating to the self-management of the behavior he is concerned about. Teach the solver chair to look for loopholes in the contract. Have the solver and problem chairs discuss ways of making the contract public so that other people can be helpful reminders for keeping the terms of the contract.

4. Have the solver and problem chairs work out a method of monitoring the current behavior, as well as expected changes, with the new self-control procedures.

5. Have the solver and problem chairs discuss ways to control the consequences of your trainee's old or new behavior in order to produce change. For ex-

ample, if he wants to change his management style of leading others by shouting at them, your trainee can ask those he manages not to respond to the shout. This environmental change takes away the old payoff for shouting.

6. Have the solver and problem chairs discuss a reward system for the desired behavior. Instruct your trainee to repeat the behavior as many times as necessary until a new habit is established. Have him discuss with himself ways to arrange his environment to increase the probability of emitting the new behavior.

Step X
Assertive Skills in Interpersonal Communications

Instructions. Furnish your trainee in the solver chair with a list of the five most frequent manipulative actions listed in Chapter 10. Have the two chairs discuss and establish the role that fits your trainee most closely. The trainee in the two-chair technique devises a plan to decelerate his frequency in the role, and instead, to develop one or more of the following assertive behaviors.

Exercise S
Assertive Skills

1. You can feel okay about yourself and others even if you don't like the others' behavior.
2. Using the two chairs, develop unexpected responses to combat invitations to be manipulated. For example, you may decide to compliment, nur-

ture, agree with, or be humorous when someone is criticizing you and wants you to feel bad rather than correct a mistake.

3. Be aware of occasions when you get into rescue roles with helpless manipulators. Develop a strategy, such as, "Sounds like you have a real problem. Hope you work it out."

4. In the solver chair, practice the formula for communicating feelings to someone close: "I feel (*state your feeling*) when you (*describe the behavior*). I want you to (*ask the desired change*)."

5. In the solver chair, ask for what you want from others, rather than hoping that they will figure it out without your asking.

6. Give positive regards to others and yourself when it is realistic.

Summary

Sometimes clients are given only a portion of the above solution training steps depending on their goals. Previously discussed in the book are criteria for the completion of solution training (see Chapter 6). My experience with clients is that they don't have enough information to set their goal for completion at the first session. However, by approximately the third to fifth session they are capable of deciding on the Basic, Intermediate, or Advanced Levels in terms of their goal. It's okay to remind them that whatever goal they have set can be changed if they decide to shoot for a higher goal later on.

One final caution: the technique in this book is by design very structured. Structure aids problem solving in providing direction, yet at the same time structure may interfere with problem solving by hampering new ideas. Feel free to deviate from the solution training structure when it is not working. Go beyond solution training when necessary to satisfy your particular need.

Bibliography

Alberti, Robert E., and Michael L. Emmons. *Your Perfect Right: A Guide to Assertive Behavior*. 2nd ed. San Luis Obispo, California: Impact, 1974.

Bandler, Richard, and John Grinder. "Meta Language" Workshop. New Orleans, 1977.

Bandler, Richard, and John Grinder. *The Structure of Magic*. Palo Alto, California: Science & Behavior Books, 1975

Baugh, J. R., G. R. Pascal, and T. B. Cottrell. "Relationship of Reported Memories of Early Experience with Parents on Interview Behavior." *Journal of Consulting and Clinical Psychology*, vol. 35 (August, 1970), pp. 23–29.

Berne, Eric. *Games People Play: The Psychology of Human Relationships*. New York: Grove Press, 1964.

Berne, Eric. *What Do You Say After You Say Hello?* New York: Grove Press, 1972.

Boyd, Harry. "Responsibility vs. Blame." *Transactional Analysis Journal*, vol. 7 (April, 1977), pp. 145–46.

Brehm, Jack W., and Arthur R. Cohen. *Explorations in Cognitive Dissonance*. New York: Wiley, 1962.

Clark, Charles H. *Brainstorming: The Dramatic New Way to Create Successful Ideas*. New York: Doubleday, 1958.

Davis, Gary A. *Psychology of Problem Solving: Theory and Practice*. New York: Basic Books, 1973.

Drucker, Peter F. "How to be an Effective Executive." *Nation's Business*, April, 1961.

Ellis, Albert, and Robert A. Harper. *A New Guide to Rational Living*. Hollywood, California: Wilshire Book Co., 1977.

Engstrom, Ted W., and Alex MacKenzie. *Managing Your Time*. Grand Rapids, Michigan: Zondervan, 1968.

Falzett, William, and Jean Maxwell. *OK Childing and Parenting*. El Paso, Texas: Transactional Analysis Institute of El Paso, 1974.

Festinger, Leon. *A Theory of Cognitive Dissonance*. Stanford, California: Stanford University Press, 1957.

Ford, G. A., and G. L. Lippitt. *Planning Your Future*. La Jolla, California: University Associates, 1972.

Freed, Alvyn M. *TA for Teens (& Other Important People)*. Sacramento, California: Jalmar Press, 1976.

Gellhorn, E. "Motion and Emotion: The Role of Proprioception in the Physiology and Pathology of Emotion." *Psychological Review*, vol. 71 (November, 1964), pp. 457–72.

Gibson, Donald L. "The Classic Non-Contract." *Transactional Analysis Journal*, vol. 4 (April, 1974), p. 31.

Gordon, William J. *Synectics*. New York: Harper & Row, 1961.

Goulding, Robert L. "Four Models of Transactional Analysis." *International Journal of Group Psychotherapy*, vol. 26 (July, 1976), pp. 385–92.

Harris, Thomas. *I'm OK, You're OK*. New York: Avon, 1976.

Hull, Clark L. *A Behavior System*. New Haven, Connecticut: Yale University Press, 1952.

James, W. "What is an Emotion?" *Mind*, 1884, 9, pp. 188–205.

Judd, Walter H. "Critique on Conflict." *Collegiate Challenge Magazine*, vol. 5 (January, 1966).

Kaufman, Roger. *Identifying and Solving Problems: A System Approach*. La Jolla, California: University Associates, 1976.

Kahler, Taibi, and H. Capers. "The Miniscript." *Transactional Analysis Journal*, vol. 4 (January, 1974).

Karpman, Steve. "Options." *Transactional Analysis Journal*, (January, 1971).

Karpman, Steve. "Script Drama Analysis." *Transactional Analysis Bulletin*, vol. 7, no. 26 (1968), pp. 39–43.

Köhler, Wolfgang. *The Mentality of Apes*. New York: Harcourt & Brace, 1925.

Laird, J. D. "The Effect of Facial Expression on an Emotional Experience." Presented at the meeting of the Eastern Psychological Association, Boston, April, 1967.

Lakein, Alan. *How to Get Control of Your Time and Your Life*. New York: David McKay, 1973.

Lowen, Alexander. *Bioenergetics*. New York: Penguin Books, 1976.

Mackenzie, R. Alec. *Time Trap*. New York: American Management Association, 1972.

Maltzman, Irving. "Thinking: From a Behavioristic Point of View." *Psychological Review*, vol. 62 (July, 1955), pp. 275–86.

Maslow, Abraham A. *Motivation and Personality*. 2nd ed. New York: Harper & Row, 1970.

Maultsby, M. "You and Your Emotion." In handout from the Psychiatric Outpatient Clinic. Lexington: University of Kentucky, 1974.

McMillan, Ryan, and B. Casey. *Talk Sense to Yourself*. Lakewood, Colorado: Jefferson County Mental Health Center, 1975.

Mittelmann, B., and H. Wolff. "Emotions and Skin Temperature: Observations on Patients During Psychotherapeutic Interviews." *Psychosomatic Medicine*, vol. 5 (1943), pp. 211–31.

Mok, Paul P. *I-Speak Your Language: A Survey of Personality Styles*. New York: Drake-Beem Associates, 1972.

Osborn, Alex F. *Applied Imagination*. Rev. ed. New York: Scribner, 1963.

Palmer, Robert D. *Advances in Behavior Therapy*. New York: Academic Press, 1973.

Phelps, Stanlee, and Nancy Austin. *The Assertive Woman*. San Luis Obispo, California: Impact, 1975.

Porter, Nancy. Personal communication.

Prince, George M. *The Practice of Creativity: A Manual for Dynamic Group Problem Solving*. New York: Harper & Row, 1970.

Razran, Gregory. "The Observable Unconscious and Inferable Conscious in Current Soviet Psychophysiology." *Psychological Review*, vol. 68 (March, 1961), pp. 81–140.

Rhinehart, Luke. *The Book of EST*. New York: Holt, Rinehart & Winston, 1976.

Satir, V. *Conjoint Family Therapy*. Palo Alto, California: Science and Behavior Books, 1964.

Scheerer, Martin. "Problem-Solving." *Scientific American*, vol. 208 (April, 1963), pp. 118–28.

Schiff, Jacqui L. *Cathexis Reader: Transactional Analysis Treatment of Psychosis*. New York: Harper & Row, 1975.

Seligman, Martin. *APA Monitor*, vol. 9 (April, 1978), p. 4

Smith, Manuel J. *When I Say No, I Feel Guilty*. New York: Dial Press, 1975.

Snyder, L. "Stroke Patterns Analysis Chart." *Transactional Analysis Journal*, vol. 8 (October, 1978).

Stampfl, T. G. "Implosive Therapy, Part I: The Theory." In S. G. Armitage, ed. *Behavior Modification Techniques and the Treatment of Emotional Disorders*. Battle Creek, Michigan: U.S. Pub., 1967.

Steiner, Claude M. *Scripts People Live: Transactional Analysis of Life Scripts*. New York: Grove Press, 1975.

Tomkins, Silvan S. *Affect, Imagery, Consciousness*. 2 vols. New York: Springer, 1962, 1963.

Wolpe, Joseph. *The Practice of Behavior Therapy*. 2nd ed. New York: Pergamon Press, 1974.

Wolpe, Joseph, and Arnold A. Lazarus. *Behavior Therapy Techniques: A Guide to the Treatment of Neuroses*. New York: Pergamon Press, 1966.